Fat Guy Runs A Marathon

By Terry Lander

Published by Lyvit Publishing, Cornwall

www.lyvit.com

ISBN 978-0-9926029-0-1

Most material was originally available on the blog, 'Fat Guy Runs A Marathon'.

“The act of running is simple, one foot in front of the other. The art of becoming a runner is achieved through a new mindset and commitment to change, especially if it’s new to you. It’s tough, challenging, painful, sometimes lonely, regularly uncomfortable and often excruciating…but the rewards are second to none.”

To my wife Mary for her patience and unwavering support and my three children, Joe, Sophie and Verity for giving up their weekend jaunts so I could go running alone.

Also to those who gave me support online and off – Paul, Arwel, Anna, Julia, Mike. Without your help and encouragement I would probably have tried slipping off without anyone noticing.

An honourable mention to the team at St John Ambulance for all the hard work you put in during the year, for the notice given to me when securing my place and, most importantly, for allowing me to run for you.

Massive thanks to anybody who read the blog and got in touch to tell me. Here it is again.

Fat Guy Runs A Marathon

Introduction

I don't run. The last time I was forced to do so was in 1998, when I was fourteen, and it was a 1500m race around the school field. My lungs burned, my legs ached and I remember thinking to myself 'what was the point of all that?'. I learned to drive as soon as I could and put a stop to the walking around I was subjected to before deciding enough was enough and I would never use my legs for anything other than moving the pedals in the car or as shoe storage devices. That was that, or so I thought.

I occasionally caught the London Marathon on TV when I moved into a house with my wife, normally during a lazy Sunday when I was still in my dressing gown eating ice-cream on the sofa. The people running didn't look like they were having any fun and the whole thing looked like a hideous chore, although I was quite comfortable so gave them some moral support from the bottom of my heart as I finished off the last of the mint choc chip.

This continued until 2006, when a good friend of mine completed the course and showed us the photo that sat proudly on her wall for all visitors to see. I even offered to go on a one mile training run with her, finding the whole experience exactly as I imagined and returning like a sweaty, basted pork loin. Something must have stirred within me however as I found myself signing up to partake at the very next opportunity despite my previous thoughts on running.

I have since concluded that my reason for signing up must have been two fold; firstly, it is notoriously difficult to get in to the London Marathon through the ballot system as they allow around 125,000 entries to the ballot, a number that is achieved well within the first day of opening, and only have 36,000 places available. Secondly, at the time, I thought applicants found out fairly quickly whether they were successful or not. Unfortunately it takes until October of the same year to find out, giving runners around six months to train and not the twelve I'd anticipated. Essentially I thought that if my number came up I'd go for it and see what came of it.

Unfortunately the first prediction came true. Year after year I applied on the day the ballot opened only to be turned down every October, possibly because I estimated that I would take quite a long time to complete the marathon. This isn't a fact, purely a theory as I could understand them wanting someone who could get round in less than a fortnight. Who wants to be marshalling deep into the evening while a chubby ice-cream chomper bounds along the roads?

I'm a peculiar person. Far from getting disheartened or even become frustrated with the ballot I took a look at my other options. I'd seen the charity places every year but looked at the minimum donations of £2,000 and was convinced I'd never be able to raise those kinds of funds in a year. As I got older and made a few close friends I started to wonder if the target was actually more achievable than I'd imagined and finally, in 2012, decided to go for it.

During the application process I asked for information from a number of charities including St John Ambulance. My Dad is heavily involved with SJA in Cornwall and their minimum donation of £1,625 seemed that much more achievable so I picked them as my first choice charity and was astounded to be given a place by May 20th, giving me a full eleven months to get training. I was advised that, should I get a ballot place, I could still run for SJA for a smaller donation of £250 but that information was essentially redundant as I once again received my 'rejected' magazine from the London Marathon. It was the first time I'd received rejection and known that I could carry on regardless, though.

So here it is, the full, unadulterated story of a fat guy going from couch to marathon and everything that's involved in the process. There may be a few gaps that I hope to fill in the editing process, although it should be noted that this is not a training guide and potential runners should get as much information from trained professionals as possible before even starting to run. There are many local running shops popping up and I would recommend using them rather than the online forums as it can be tough to gauge your level and information from elite athletes is unlikely to be applicable to most runners.

Most importantly I found a consistent training plan that I found comfortable and it kept me running. I may have achieved a better time had I put more time into running but I may also have ended up with no family. Everybody's different and circumstances change. This is simply how I went about it.

Kit List

Running trainers x 3
Running socks x 3
Shorts
Cycling shorts
Sweat bands
Armband for phone
Plasters
Vaseline
T-Shirts
Long sleeved T-Shirts
Gels
Running Belt
Lightweight coat
Snacks
Tracking software for phone
Suncream

For after long runs

Gloves
Hat
Jumper
Trousers

A Note About Fundraising

I seem to have glossed over the auction in the following pages despite the fact the fundraising was what put me off getting a charity place for so many years. In truth, I worried for a long time that I wouldn't get anywhere near my £1625 target and started saving like mad just in case I had to make up the deficit. I spent many a night writing down ideas and told everyone I met that I was running in the hope they'd put forward some funds as I'm not one to ask directly.

For those needing to raise funds for a charity I would definitely recommend an auction. I was lucky enough to get some great lots but a large number of small lots will help to achieve the same result. As mentioned earlier there were only five people present at the time the auction was meant to start, 7.00pm, and that included my wife, myself and the auctioneer. We delayed the start as it would have been completely pointless to begin and the lots would likely have gone for a pound each. We eventually got wind that a few other friends were planning to get to us just after 8.00pm, which is why we started at 8.30pm. Even then there were only around 20 guests and we were panicking about the target being reached.

From 7.00pm – 8.30pm we were starting to discuss other fundraising ideas as I was certain we would have to put something else on. The ideas suggested were a pub quiz, bake sale, car boot sale, non-uniform day at a local school, themed disco, car wash and barbeque. Luckily for me the lots we had were sufficient for a £1200 total and I didn't really need to do anything else. I probably should have, yet the stress of the auction put me off trying to get groups of people together and I opted for keeping a sponsor form on me at all times.

Along with the auction we held a raffle and a couple of the guests offered to have their legs waxed, helping the total to grow without too much extra effort. Combining ideas in this way saves having to get a crowd together for a second or third time. It's also useful to have buckets or collection tins handy as people are generally happy to get rid of their loose change, particularly for a good cause.

As well as fundraising events it seems vital to set up an online donation page for which I used JustGiving, although being in the Virgin London Marathon I perhaps should have used Virgin Giving. In truth they are very similar and the end result is that donations can be gift-aided and are sent straight to the charity. This saves fundraisers having to chase and collate money or send funds from their own accounts.

It's tough to get donations from strangers although I tried social networking and had a lot of support from the online community. Twitter was perhaps my best source but that had a lot to do with retweets from Al Murray, Robin Ince, Tiernan Douieb and Adam Kay (who also ran the London Marathon for St John Ambulance, although his place was confirmed in the January before so he had much less time to train!). People with large follower numbers can get your message to the most people, however they are also bombarded with requests so it's best not to ask them more than once. St John Ambulance themselves have a Twitter account and seemed to be more than happy to help by retweeting my messages so it's always best to try your charity first.

The most important thing to remember is that a marathon is a massive challenge and most people will be more than willing to put their hand in their pocket to support runners. I was amazed that I reached my target by the 3rd of November as I was certain I'd have to go door to door selling hand-made cakes, however I would have done it in the pouring rain if that's what it took to get me to London. Above all be positive about your actions and show people you will work hard for donations as it mirrors the hard work you need to put in to the running.

From The Blog

SUNDAY, 20 MAY 2012

First Run

I've received an email from St John Ambulance welcoming me to the team. This means, should I not be successful in the ballot in October, I will still get to run the 2013 London Marathon. This is unfortunate.

To give a bit of background, the last time I ran I was fourteen. It was a Sports Day at school and we were advised to run to boost our house's chances of winning the day. We got a point for taking part. It felt like I was being attacked the whole time and I came second to last, mainly because myself and another lad were having a chat.

Fourteen years on and I've acquired a reputation for laziness. I once got a thin plank of wood to turn the TV off in my room as it didn't have a remote. I'm the first one into the biscuits and the last one out. My only real reason for running the marathon is to stop people telling me they want to run the marathon one day. I believe it will give me the superhuman ability to turn my nose up and chuckle smugly.

I'm very self conscious in that I hate people seeing me in a state of discomfort. I would never have joined a gym as it involves fit people moving machines with ease while I struggle with a tiny weight and sweat a lot. This was the biggest problem I've had to overcome today as I took to the road for the first time and felt the tarmac beneath my feet.

There was no fanfare and nobody stopped to congratulate me yet my fears were unfulfilled, too. The cars drove past and I recognised someone I knew who either didn't see me or chose to ignore me. I didn't really care. I then saw someone I knew from work who beeped repeatedly and shouted "Do some running" as I was flicking between walking and running as suggested. My embarrassment was nowhere to be seen as I laughed, knowing I'll see him tomorrow and make some remark before telling him why I was doing it.

As promised, on my return my shins ached like mad and my body was tight (steady, ladies - I'm taken) but I found, although I didn't enjoy it as such, it was good to make it home. I now have 11 months of training in which I need to buy better trainers, better socks and an mp3 player to keep my training manageable.

This is no sports advert for sure. I have not become one with running. I do believe I will achieve my aim, though. Who cares if people laugh?

MONDAY, 21 MAY 2012

Maniacal Laughing

As predicted, my workmates find the idea of me running the London Marathon hilarious. Some were almost on the floor with laughter at their mental image of my chubby frame wobbling along the course with the crew of St John Ambulance spending the money I've raised scraping me off the pavement before I'd made the start line. There's nothing quite like support from your peers to keep your motivation high.

My training plan naturally has a lot of rest days. Currently I'm on three days training, four days of rest. The fact that I am on a rest day today sent them over the edge as they came close to involuntarily releasing their bowels over the floor and had to hold on to each other to stand up. Every day, they suggested, is a rest day for me.

If you were in any doubt that I am a fat guy running a marathon I hope this helps to sway your decision.

MONDAY, 21 MAY 2012

...But Why?

People have been asking me all day why I'm running the marathon. Not just with an inquisitive tone, more of a '...but why in the hell are you running a marathon?!'

I've never been in to running or considered a shorter course, so I thought back six years to when I first applied to determine the answer for myself. To be honest, I struggled to come up with an answer. There is the whole 'once in a lifetime experience' idea which best fits my reason, so I may start telling people that. I'm pretty sure that once the run is over with I won't be going back to do it again.

I love the idea of going from dead still to marathon. In a way it's an experiment as, if I finish, no-one will ever have an excuse not to give it a go should they really want to. It would be impossible for people to say 'I would do it, but I could never get fit' as the proof is in the pudding shaped man.

On a brighter note, I was told to get good socks (which was also laughed at this morning by my workmates) so my good lady wife bought me these this morning:

A good pair of trainers are next on the list. My wife is helping a lot with getting me out on the road training and fundraising, so if I'm asked to give a speech at the end I will sure to say 'Thhhhhh...thaaa...mmmmmmm...ahh, my legs... bluuuuuuuuuuugh' before I pass out.

WEDNESDAY, 23 MAY 2012

Dietary Advice

Now that it's sunk into people's minds that I will be running and they've told me to take it easy with my training, dietary advice is starting to be thrown my way. Naturally I have listened and nodded as I don't want to appear rude but I have already considered altering my diet slowly to accommodate my new increase in activity.

I've also booked in to see my doctor for a medical to make sure I have no problems, bodily speaking. They'll probably say I'm fat and should lose weight but I can at least expect that. If they give me dietary advice and tell me to take it easy while I'm training I may pop.

It's not that I don't appreciate the advice - I've got new trainers, new socks and a doctor's appointment off the back of such advice - it's more that I'm getting contradictory advice from different sources. If you know your stuff and can provide tried and tested methods of achieving a goal then feel free to come forward and provide it. However, if you've read in a newspaper or heard from a relative that eating chicken causes runners to peck at the ground, please keep it to yourself.

This could probably be applied to other situations in life, too...

Thanks to Paul and Arwel on Twitter for the advice and support so far, it's been above and beyond the call of duty. Both have been running for long enough for me to know their advice is sound. Also thanks to Mike, Anna and Julia for the support.

THURSDAY, 24 MAY 2012

Mixing It Up

As well as training with runs I'm still playing six-a-side football to give me some variation during the week. Also I love playing football, which helps. I'm sure there are many out there who would be concerned about my risk of injury but I try not to move too much during a game (which makes me a terrible player, yet I'm comfortable with that) and stick to doing what I'm good at.

I will pretty much play football any time, anywhere and I feel now like I've worked so much more of my entire body, not just the parts I need for the marathon. I only have six games to go this season though, after which I will more than likely need to take up running on a Thursday as well. I have yet to find out how I will feel about this, however it's all part of the experience.

Perhaps next season I'll turn out a little fitter and I'll actually be able to contribute to the game rather than standing around and hoping the ball comes near me. Maybe I'm not as bad as that despite feeling it during some matches. I certainly won't be on the six figure weekly salaries any time soon, though.

I never did get back to football the next season as our manager had no enthusiasm from our team. A real shame.

THURSDAY, 24 MAY 2012

Good Advice

I've had some good advice from Helen Squire, who is a veteran runner and has been through the London Marathon experience recently. Here it is, verbatim:

"My first tip to anyone is join a running club with a good coach. Our club - Mounts Bay Harriers - is excellent and has a brilliant coach with lots of experience and would devise a training plan. Build distance gradually. Cross train, eat healthily and also programme in recovery days. Speed training and hill training are also important - the short sessions are as important as long sessions. Another tip is find a running partner to help motivation and keep you going - which is where joining a running club can help - they're all like minded nutters! Buy 'Runners World' magazine - full of tips and inspiration. Programme in other shorter races, which create a good atmosphere and get you used to what to expect"

This week has been incredible for receiving advice and it's important to know who to trust. Helen has been there, seen it and done it whereas many of those giving me advice are speculating or have read something in a newspaper. I appreciate everybody's input but now I feel more confident that I'm on the right path. This one has a gingerbread house, for example. One second, there's a lady coming out of it. I didn't think she was in but she's...

SATURDAY, 26 MAY 2012

Third Run

Running is hard. When you don't do it very often, it's particularly hard. I do like getting back though. The specific muscles that ache during my runs have gone from shins to calves and now, thighs. I'm hoping this means I'm building from the bottom up rather than changing my running style, although I can't be sure.

I had to go today instead of tomorrow as it's my third and youngest child's party tomorrow afternoon and I have an awful feeling I'm going to be busy. I also want to make sure I'm available as I don't think my wife will appreciate me literally running out of the door when it all kicks off. This means I had to run during a busy session on the road and the cars refuse to give way to pedestrians no matter how fat we are. I got by, though, and we seemed to mutually respect each others' section of the road in that I didn't venture too close to the white line.

Yesterday I had to move 34 bags of stones to go into a new parking space and I may have overdone it slightly. This may have been why I was feeling a little lethargic at each stage of my run (before, during and after) and also the reason I had to walk a little more than I have done before. This effectively means a higher amount of traffic saw a reduced amount of running. At least I could appease my own sense of satisfaction regardless of the potential judging (I believe they refer to it as 'paranoia' in psychological circles).

Now I can relax at my daughter's birthday party knowing I've completed my required weekend training. I'm hoping to get a leg rub later on as well. I might have to do it myself, though.

SATURDAY, 26 MAY 2012

Pins And Needles: Update

I have pins and needles in my legs.

TUESDAY, 29 MAY 2012

Slight Problem

There's been a bit of a mix up. Being an electrician, I often have to measure rooms and cables before fitting to ensure they...well, fit. With this in mind, when I was asked to run 26.2m I thought it would be easy. Peoples' posting of times between 3-6 hours seemed comical as I can walk 26.2 metres in just a few minutes. When someone pointed out to me that the 'm' means miles I had no choice but to freak out. It seems these thirty second jogs I've been doing have been of no use at all and I have revised my training plan to include some slightly longer runs. This isn't true, but it did occur to me today that it may have been a possibility. Now I'm concerned that 'm' doesn't mean miles, perhaps it means motorways. 26.2 motorways. I'll have to check.

While I was out for a run today I noticed another jogger on the same route and perked myself up a bit so I didn't look too knackered as I passed him. Last year I went to Bath to play in a cricket tournament with a bunch of lads, most of whom I knew from various departments around where I work. It turned out the jogger was a guy who accompanied us to that tournament, so it was doubly important that I took steps to stop him from calling me an ambulance. I'm still building my confidence in this area as I pass fitter and more experienced athletes, although I also realise that everyone has to start somewhere and this is essentially my starting point.

My next training event is six-a-side football this Thursday. However, I have my medical to come tomorrow so tune in then to see if I make it through.

WEDNESDAY, 30 MAY 2012

Post Medical

I have been to see a nurse. This is a big step as she could have told me I'm in massive peril and can't run next April. Unfortunately she suggested I'm a big fat guy and should probably run twice just to be sure. Luckily I'm fairly tall as it balances out my circular appearance.

Herein lies the problem; apparently, according to my ideal weight, I'm a person and a half. To be in a position where I don't have to hide how happy I am I need to lose a third of my weight. BMI charts are controversial as muscle weighs more than fat and therefore they don't take in to account particularly fit individuals, however I'm in no position to claim immunity as I have a very high Crisp : Exercise ratio.

My intention was never to actually lose weight during the course of my training, although I knew it would be a bi-product. I said from the start I'd be happy to put all the weight back on afterwards as I'm happy in who I am and can take the odd fat joke every twenty seconds. However, this has put things into perspective a little and given me an actual figure to aim for with my weight loss as well as being able to go the distance. Whether I keep it down or not after the event is up to me then as I don't want to think a future me, who has been running and lifting weights, will want to come back and find me for making unrealistic goals that he has to achieve.

If any of this doesn't make sense, I suggest you go back into the past and read more Dr. Seuss. "For if there's no sense then you may as well cease, but the gist of the post is I'm rather obese".

FRIDAY, 1 JUNE 2012

Exhaustion

For the first time in my training I'm really feeling the effects of having done perhaps a touch too much. We had a particularly hard game last night and we played out of our skins just to lose six-nil, which we knew would be the case. I have been outside this afternoon to do some gardening (which I detest with a passion) and have found my shoulders ache, my back is throbbing and my thighs are stiff and therefore useless.

My next run will have to be on Sunday as I'm not sure I could move it forward to the Saturday this week, however it means I have to go bowling soon after running and don't know if I'll be able to stand up. I may just leave it until the time and see how I feel, perhaps with a view to running in the morning so I get a decent bit of rest in between.

I was told before I started that it was a big commitment and I have found a routine I can stick to quite well, although it's important for me not to miss any training so early into my regime as I'm likely to suffer as a result. I have been toying with the idea of two runs at the weekend, both shorter routes, though I need to extend my Sunday runs when I get closer to the event so I shelved that idea. More isn't always better, particularly when you're nursing a body like mine.

SATURDAY, 2 JUNE 2012

Cross Training: Issues

I took a look at my bike earlier with a view to going out on it, keeping my training fresh and exciting as planned. However, both tyres are flat and the brakes are rusty, issues which can be resolved but not immediately. I have four tyres in the garden but they are designed to fit a Ford Mondeo and don't look anything like the right size.

On the plus side I've ordered an mp3 player to provide some background music during my runs. I'll have to be careful when I fill it with songs as I find it hard to get pumped when Paul Weller is playing 'You do something to me' in my ear. I'm unlikely to upload 'Eye of the tiger' either as it's too much of a cliché and I would hate for people to drive past me and think "Ah, it's been done".

SUNDAY, 3 JUNE 2012

The Shins Are King

I've just been out on my normal Sunday route and, around 3/4 of the way round, my shins started aching more than usual. I've made it my mantra to listen to my body throughout my training and during the marathon and to respond accordingly so I took longer than usual to warm down and I've stretched my shins for an extra few minutes. The most important thing for me is to get around the whole course regardless of what time I finish in.

On a side note a number of people have noticed that I appear to have lost weight. This is despite maintaining my former dietary regime which has proven a lot to me. A couple of years ago I stopped eating from the massive tins of chocolates that are rife at Christmas as I knew they were empty calories and seemed addictive. This year I stopped eating the biscuits that are brought into work, which only reduces my intake by about 7 a week yet seemed again to be more out of habit than needing a snack.

Since making those changes I've managed to keep my weight at about the same level but don't think I have ever really lost anything. However, since starting to run twice a week and keeping the football up on a Thursday I've had a good few compliments followed by the ego busting "...but you're still just as ugly" remarks. Hey, there's no point getting a big head this early in the game.

TUESDAY, 5 JUNE 2012

Row, row, row your rowing machine

Following my shin problems I decided to jump on the rowing machine. I bought it about two years ago from a workmate for twenty five quid and only ever used it for sporadic ten minute stints during Rory and Paddy's Great British Adventure on a Monday. Since I moved six months ago, however, I haven't used it at all.

I've always had a really tough relationship with my back (we once went a whole week without talking) so I was careful to adopt a posture that wouldn't aggravate it any further which isn't as easy as it sounds. Also going from ten minutes to thirty minutes is something of a step but, with the help of some music and half the water supply I actually needed, I got through and it was enjoyable towards the end. I don't know if rowing will be helpful to my overall goal but I figured some exercise is better than none and it helped to strengthen my thighs. I will pose that question and update it here later.

During the rowing a piece fell off the machine and I almost soiled my trousers thinking it may have been a supporting bracket or a weight before noticing one of the end caps roll past me with a wink and a smile. That's not the kind of incident I need during my training as I'm still delicate despite being so chunky.

I finished my session in time for the intro to Queen's 'One Vision', which was quite rewarding. Having a band as big as that playing their biggest opening at the end of your session is very flattering. Even Freddie came along. I know I can't have that for every session but the memories will last forever.

TUESDAY, 5 JUNE 2012

Psychics

I have an answer. I asked two people, independently, whether the rowing machine was any good for cross training and they both said the same thing - yes it is, so take the coats off it and start using it. Other Twitter users have also confirmed its usefulness in building upper body strength and endurance while, as predicted, being better than doing nothing or eating honey sandwiches in front of the tennis.

Last night's football went better than expected. We were playing against a Helston Sports Centre team and took the lead, after which they overtook us before we pulled it back to 3-2. By the end of the match we were hanging off the railings and could barely talk, but we finished eventual losers at 5-2. The fact that I never post match results on here should be an indication of how well we played against six individuals who spend most of their time in the gym, although I'm suffering with my back this morning. Oh, my aching back.

FRIDAY, 8 JUNE 2012

Official Medical Verdict

When I first rang my surgery to book a medical, as suggested by so many, they didn't know who to book me in to see - the doctor or the nurse. I picked the nurse because I needed my bloods doing anyway (I have an under active Thyroid) and was told upon arrival that she couldn't do a sufficient enough medical and I would need to see the doctor.

Today I saw a doctor who told me I needn't have booked in with them unless I had a particular problem that may have needed consultation. Although she didn't directly tell me I'd wasted an appointment I had, in effect, wasted an appointment. That said, I now know my fatty cholesterol is slightly high, my blood pressure is normal and my heart and lungs are fine. "If anything", I was told, "training can really only benefit you". Sounds familiar.

If you decide to take up running, here are some things I've learned.

Get good trainers and good socks. Never, ever, ever scrimp - if you're going running you absolutely have to pay a lot for trainers and get checked out on these new fangled machines that measure your running gait. There are no ifs or buts. That said, £100 for a pair of trainers opens up a sport that is just about free thereafter.

Listen to your body. If you ache, rest. If you ache for a long time, get it checked out.

Change your diet. It's one thing to pummel yourself into the ground chasing a thinner you but pointless if you get back on the KFC every night. Do it slowly so that you don't miss the foods you cut out and if you do start to fancy something, have it. Perhaps pick a favourite though.

Do it because you want to. If people call you fat and you want to prove them wrong, you'll quit. If you want to look like Angelina Jolie, you'll quit. If you start to feel good about running and take in a few sights then you may just stay on course.

Get a running partner with similar aims. You'll help each other out and drag each other to the park on wet days. If you can't find anyone straight away, chances are you'll catch up with someone in the future once you're confident in your abilities.

Naturally I am writing this to keep you updated on things I learn along the way so feel free to check back regularly. None of this is rocket science but it's good to have a pool of 'first offs' to ensure you stay healthy.

MONDAY, 11 JUNE 2012

Bath In June

It looks like my Tuesday runs are going to have to make way for Cricket training as I'm due in Bath in three weeks for a six-a-side tournament. I'm not a Cricket person but when I'm such a vital component (substitute number two - hopefully I won't have to play too much) I can't say no.

Well, I could say no, yet I'm certain I'd get bundled into a van and tied into a room for two nights. Besides, Bed and Breakfast for £25 is an absolute steal. Let's go to Bath.

TUESDAY, 12 JUNE 2012

Re-Shuffle

No sooner than the cricket training had been confirmed, the heavens opened and soaked everything from pitches to nets with torrential style rain that made wet rain look merely moist. I was looking for some rain training and decided to go back to my original plan, although the rain had passed by the time I went out and the only real difference was the amount of standing water on the ground; still a potential hazard, though not enough to really alter my route.

I tried for a new milestone in my running and reached the two mile mark, which is a gentle step up but still challenging for someone of my physique. The rowing yesterday didn't seem to interfere with my running as my legs felt fresh and, post run, were still in good shape. It seems my shins have been sufficiently rested to allow me to run as normal which is encouraging for similar situations in the future.

Running in the countryside gives me access to a great view and I can see Loe Bar from the road, which is a band of sand dividing a small pool from the sea. I also caught sight of a fox as I was jogging, although the cute little bunny jiggling in it's jaws made it somewhat less appealing. Sights like that stop me from heading to the gym and I'm hoping that will still be the case when I'm caught in the downpours as mentioned earlier.

I'm also hoping this will be my last session in cheap trainers as I'm booked in to At Your Pace in Helston, a specialist running shop with all the latest technology. Being a size 12 makes it somewhat awkward as they have to order my shoes in but it's a small price to pay for having giant standing equipment.

THURSDAY, 14 JUNE 2012

Magic Shoes

It finally happened. I made an appointment with the good people at At Your Pace in Helston (Behind Tyacke Road car park) and was taken through the measuring of the gait to be fitted with a pair of Saucony Omni 10 running shoes. The staff at AYP are amazing and, I was told the second I took my shoes and socks off, I have been buying size 12's for years despite being a size 11. This is because my feet are very wide and barely fit in a normal size 11, something I must have compensated for all those years ago. This meant I was fitted for the right shoes straight away and was given others to try that they knew would be too big or small - they really, really know their stuff.

They're also confident even a big guy like me can get into running and complete the marathon, although my build stops me putting in competitive times. This is good as I have no intention of trying; I'm in, run, out. Ironically my build is probably suited to rugby but my lack of competitive spirit puts me out of any team. That and my weight. Also my stamina.

As I left I was given some nutritional information and was pointed towards a calendar of races that I will try to peruse soon. Failing that I have one in mind that I need to apply for, so fingers crossed that will be my first event. The marathon is a long way off and I feel I have given myself the best chance of completing it, particularly now that I have support for those less-than-massive-but-still-big leg ends down there.

I've said it before and I'll say it again - spend good money on your shoes. Your feet are the ones doing the hard work so treat them right.

SUNDAY, 17 JUNE 2012

Another First Run

I got out there earlier in my new shoes and the difference is phenomenal. I can feel the cushioning in the areas that have extra and the road feels like a mattress beneath my feet. I also plugged in the mp3 player and that took my mind off the silence and occasional engine noise that passed which combined to offer a new experience.

I'm still tuning in to running having done very little before but I can feel my recovery getting so much better and my body becoming tighter with every mile I put in. I'm now logging each run so I know when it's time to get a new pair of trainers which is particularly important for professional shoes.

Most importantly I have grown in confidence and couldn't care less if people see me walking at intervals or running in a peculiar way. I look at the scenery as I run and people have commented that I don't wave as they drive past but I'm more than happy to if they put hand to horn, after which I will divert my attention back to the scenery. No one else matters when I'm out there as I'm the one who has to put in 26.2 miles next year and, by that time, I'll be a new person.

I've got great support from my family and I know not everyone has this commodity, however everybody has themselves to answer to and if you're not happy with your level of fitness I would implore you to get out and take a walk once in a while. I never used to bother and complained about my body shape occasionally yet I am now happy with how things are going and it all started with a push from myself.

Forgive me for the greetings card style emotional post. Just be glad I didn't end with 'you can do it'.

I soon ditched the mp3 player as it made me too nervous, particularly while I was running along the roads. This turned out to be a great idea as it meant I wasn't dependant on technology to go running. "Oh no, my battery's flat. No running for me today."

WEDNESDAY, 20 JUNE 2012

Cricket Training

Yesterday my cricket training took place and, judging by the pain in my legs, it's not a bad exercise for my training. It wasn't quite enough (cricket is quite a gentle game if you ignore the 90mph solid balls, believe it or not) so I jumped on the rowing machine to beef up my overall training.

It wasn't easy fitting it in - I had to take my son to his guitar lesson, jump onto the rowing machine, jump off and take my daughter to pick up my son before I dropped them both off to another club. I then went to watch the England game. This is proof that there was always time in my life, but never the motivation; this is slowly changing with each session.

A big problem I've come across is hydration so I've bought a case load of water bottles and left them all over the house, ready for filling at any point. Obviously this has effects at the other end but that's not really an issue. I have to remember to drink while I'm running, particularly on the long runs, and take some small snacks or energy gels/drinks to keep my sugar levels constant. This advice was given to me by the good people from At Your Pace in Helston, which means it is solid advice.

FRIDAY, 22 JUNE 2012

Super Oops

Something bad has happened. Last night, during our scheduled six-a-side game, I endured a heavily paced ball to the head and suffered concussion. On believing I was alright this morning I attempted to jump a wall that I have jumped many times in the past only to find my balance was still off and I landed on my shins. It hurt immensely, needless to say my first ever scheduled Saturday run will not happen tomorrow as I recover from the after effects of concussion and an entire body to the shins.

Although this hasn't put me back as such it has impeded on my new schedule. I am taking the rough with the smooth, however, by putting my feet up immediately with a cup of tea and resting for 36 hours.

SUNDAY, 24 JUNE 2012

Gentle exercise

After a weekend of falling over I was advised not to go for a run today so took to the exercise bike for a gentle ride. I spent an hour watching a Fatboy Slim DVD and circling my legs, going nowhere but getting fit and having a good time.

I bought myself some shorts last week and jumped into a pair today to find they're quite tight, so if you see a jogger at the side of the road and can see every vein and scar then be sure to beep and wave. Also think about me when you get home and be sure to upload a donation online.

I'll be putting together a fundraising event in August and have a lot to organise before we get there, however if you have something kicking around that might do well (or badly) in an auction then please email me at trjl@hotmail.com. All donations gratefully received.

I never did get much donated online, I had to go out to businesses and call on every contact I had individually. It's hard work but well worth the effort.

WEDNESDAY, 27 JUNE 2012

Annual Bath (Trip)

Today's the day I go to Bath for the cricket tournament, which means from next Tuesday I can get back to running. There's a chance I may be able to enter a 1500m run in Bath if it doesn't coincide with the cricket so I'm keeping my fingers crossed.

I'm really starting to miss running as I was building up a good routine and tempo, however I couldn't let my cricket colleagues down by not turning up - far better to turn up and let them down with my terrible batting and laughable bowling styles.

The fundraising event in August has evolved and is now a charity auction and disco in September. It's all booked up and I'm now looking for items to auction off which gives me an air of constantly asking people for something, whether it be money or items. Still, it's for a good cause.

SATURDAY, 30 JUNE 2012

The Beginning Of The Beginning

The good news is I made the 1500m race in Bath. The great news is I finished it. This means I have my first set of numbers.

My time is not worth mentioning, suffice it to say that I didn't come last and I'm very happy with that. Furthermore, my cricketing colleagues made the final of the cricket so couldn't be there to watch me. This is even better as it's proven I can run in front of strangers without support for the best part of a mile. The next challenge is plugging the gap between mile 1 and mile 26.

It's highlighted the importance of keeping up the training as, although I have been exercising, I hadn't actually run for nearly two weeks. While I was going round the track I felt tired and really noticed the lack of use in my muscles, hopefully a lasting inspiration for my training. I have no extra-curricular events between now and the marathon and should be able to stick with the regime that was working so well for me before.

I may have tried to keep pace with the front runners when I started the race but I soon found my own rhythm and stopped thinking about how many were in front of me. Most of the other entrants looked sporty when compared to me and could clearly waltz 1500m without too much fuss - in fact, one guy had finished a 5k race half an hour before taking part. The people behind me made me feel a touch better, yet things would be no different if I'd pulled myself in right at the back. Somebody has to come last.

For me the guy who came last was the one who pulled off after two laps, roughly 800m. He *really* made me feel good about my run.

SUNDAY, 1 JULY 2012

Back To Training

Tonight I went for my first run since competing (two whole days ago) and found my legs were very stiff afterwards, probably due to the fact it was road running as opposed to running on the track. I was always told road running was tough and I'm appreciating it now but I refuse to give up.

I've also started collecting items for my auction as I'm still a good way off my target for fundraising. Training and fundraising are taking over my life currently but I'm glad to be a part of it, particularly given the amount of time I have to complete both. I'm grateful to all those who have contributed so far and my readers, so thanks again to all involved.

TUESDAY, 3 JULY 2012

S'Raining

I was the only person in the UK glad to see the rain as it gave me a chance to get out running in it. As I was told by the guys at At Your Pace in Helston, the bulk of my training will be during the cold, harsh winter months and it's quite likely to rain during that time. I was quite surprised at how much I enjoyed running in the rain, although if I'm honest it was because it was more of a drizzle and meant I didn't have to run beneath the hot, relentless sun.

As a glasses wearer I clearly have another issue to deal with when it rains aside from the possible slips, trips and falls (as dictated by the health and safety manual). I had to give them a bit of a wipe after each mile but, if it rains during the marathon, that's only 26 wipes. Give or take a few.

It was also my first run with someone else, a guy I work with who's been running for a while and had to wait for me to catch up. I'm guessing this didn't put him off as we're booked in to run again on Friday, although he's not quite so keen to run in the rain. If the bad weather's still about on Friday I may have to go solo again.

THURSDAY, 5 JULY 2012

The End Of Football

The local six-a-side football season has come to an end so I have three choices; do I run on the Thursday, Friday or both from now on? This is clearly a rhetorical question as I'm hoping to go out tomorrow if I don't feel too bad from the football and, in future, I will take each week as it comes to see which is the best day and whether I can fit both in comfortably.

I may try to up my mileage tomorrow as I felt I could have done last Tuesday, however it's better for me to take a short run if I'm tired than try to push myself so that's what I'll aim for to begin with. It'll be a solo run as my temporary running partner is off with a bad case of the birthdays. It sounds unfortunate and I wish him well.

FRIDAY, 6 JULY 2012

New Milestone

The questions about my weight and time still flood in but it's the distance I'm measuring and I can now run two and a half miles comfortably, although I didn't have time to shower before going back to work and I smelled like an old chair for the afternoon. This is the risk you take when running in a dinnertime.

It felt good to get back to the car and still have the energy for the extra half mile despite a small niggle threatening to develop during my run. I also had a bit of company as I was running my final leg, my confidence taking a small dip as I was overtaken by another guy. I felt somewhat better when I read the words 'Iron Man, Switzerland' on the back of his top, reminding me that it's my pace that matters and no-one else's.

If only I could convince myself more often.

SATURDAY, 7 JULY 2012

Fundraising

There's nothing worse than hearing people bleat on about how you should give to charity. There are so many charities out there and people are really struggling to find funds to maintain their own lifestyles, so why should we put our hands in our pockets when money is so tight?

I should make a bold statement here about how charities need us more when money is tight but I'm not going to. All I will say is that I need to raise another £1,505 to make all of this training worthwhile, otherwise the marathon organisers will tell me to take my training and be a bit lighter without allowing me on to their gruelling circuit to kick the hell out of my aching limbs.

I reckon there must be at least 2-3,000 people on the internet, so if everyone reading this gave a pound then I'd be well on my way to achieving my target. I'm even fairly certain I will never run the marathon again, so this is literally a once in a lifetime opportunity to say "Here, fatso. Have a pound. Now go and ruin your ankles."

I would be so unbelievably grateful.

I'm fully aware that there are more than 3,000 people on the internet. Don't worry for my sanity.

SUNDAY, 8 JULY 2012

Making The Most Of It

The great thing about cross training is that you get to use different muscles and tone your body in a way that helps to reduce injuries as well as keeping training interesting. More importantly it means that, if you're watching the Wimbledon final on TV and don't have time to fit in a run, you can drag out the bike and stick an hour of training on top of the tennis.

The bike is probably the least effective form of training I've done, however it's good for my thighs and calves and at least got me sweating. This week I'm planning three runs and a half hour rowing machine session to compliment my tennis watching.

As ever, if you see me at the side of the road be sure to give me a beep.

TUESDAY, 10 JULY 2012

Just Another Runny Tuesday

My work colleague got over his bout of the birthdays and came out with me again. We achieved a comfortable three mile run (each, not between us) and I have some plans for training this week. They mainly involve running, rowing and cycling - not necessarily in that order.

This could be a short post. Yep, it is.

Although I could mention my niggles. No, I won't.

THURSDAY, 12 JULY 2012

Cream Cakecercise

Where I work it's tradition to have a cake on Fridays. No ifs, no buts. Cake. This week it was my turn to buy them so I took to the supermarket to buy four boxes worth which were piled on top of each other as I walked to the checkout. On the way I noticed one of my old P.E. teachers, although it wasn't one of those who accepted me as the tubby child I once was (and still, technically, am). It was the type who likes to teach children the benefit of P*A*I*N.

He must have felt defeated to see me as an adult, cake boxes piled high, walking past him. What he didn't realise was that my evening involved thirty minutes on a rowing machine without a single drop of cream. Had I felt the urge to talk to him I would have chuckled 'these aren't all for me' before giving a cheeky wink and paying for them. As it is I wasn't a fan of P*A*I*N so I didn't bother to fill him in. I put my nose in the air and gave him a look that said 'these ARE all for me'.

I suppose I could still eat them all as they're in the fridge. I might not, though.

FRIDAY, 13 JULY 2012

Gentle Jog

I took myself and my running partner for a two mile jogette this afternoon under a cool, cloudy sky. We even managed to find some other runners who acknowledged our existence. Which is super.

Running can be a very solitary activity and most people are pushing their bodies when they encounter others, but surely a nod isn't an impossibility. It's also really hard to judge which runners will say hello and which would push you into the ground given half a chance, unlike people walking past who generally give a little gesture of greeting before they continue on their way.

I'm thinking of having T-Shirts printed for runners with their average reaction to other runners so I can take the guesswork out of these meetings. It might save me getting my head stamped on.

MONDAY, 16 JULY 2012

Logistics

I encountered a small problem over the weekend in that I had no running trousers and had to take to the bike, my legs not being in a condition where I can legally take them out exposed under a pair of shorts. I should have bought new trousers by now but the truth is I haven't. That's me being completely honest and open with you all. An hour on the bike is no less helpful to my overall training so at least I can rest on that factette.

Another problem I have is this; when I go running on a Tuesday I have a set amount of time in which to complete said running. Three miles takes me to about the limit, however Tuesdays were the day I was extending my runs. I now have to try and take longer runs on a Sunday which is much more likely to have other events contained within it, such as the birthday party yesterday. I'm getting to the point where I have to decline invites and it's something I knew would come but never really wanted to admit to myself.

If you're reading this and having a party in the coming months, please hold it on a Friday after my midday run as there is more of a chance I can attend. Naturally I'll try and fit everyone in but I can't promise.

Just as importantly I've set up the text service on JustGiving, so you can now donate as little as £1 by texting LYVT99 and the amount (eg LYVT99 £1). I've reached 8% of my goal, much more than expected, yet it's made me hungry for more donations. If 1465 people donate £1 today I'll be set up for the run.

THURSDAY, 19 JULY 2012

Milestone Alert

I forgot to mention that on Tuesday that I ran three and a half miles, my longest distance to date. I was going to celebrate tonight with a row but I seem to have caught a flu bug and am trying to sweat it out as I type. If it continues I'll end up missing my midday run tomorrow so I'm drugged up on flu tablets and drinking water like it's my last hope.

On the other hand I've had some great lots coming in for my auction in September. It should be a good one and hopefully I'll raise quite a bit towards my target. It'll be one less thing to worry about then.

TUESDAY, 24 JULY 2012

Illness Issues

My friend had a surprise party at the weekend; well, we had one for her at my place. This gave me the freedom to drink as much as I required before waking up on some area of floor somewhere without worrying that I was disturbing an unforgiving relative. Fortunately I made it to bed, however on Sunday I woke up with the biggest, most painful bout of tonsillitis ever.

I've had it before, particularly last year when I had four bouts, but it has put a bit of a stop to the training as I've been prescribed lots of rest and fluids. I'm concerned about whether this will put me back, although At Your Pace in Helston told me that if I miss training I should continue with my plan and not go back to sessions I haven't achieved.

I'm hoping to be better on Friday as it will be in time for my short run, however last Sunday I was hoping to put a good few miles under the shoes so I will have to try and do that this week. It's not going back; essentially I was looking at extending my Sunday runs as I have no time restrictions.

I was also looking at a race for when we go to Wales in August but it'll have finished by the time we get there and I don’t think I can leave any earlier. I will be running in Wales, I just won't get any race experience. However the rewards are there as the Red Lion in Machynlleth is a fantastic place to drink. I just hope I don't get tonsillitis from the beer again.

FRIDAY, 27 JULY 2012

I Beat Tonsillitis

It's been exactly a week since I last did any training and I still have the raspy throat from my week long illness so I was apprehensive before going into my training about how much I could actually manage. I aimed for one mile, allowed myself two and let my body decide on the facts. I was also carrying a bit of a calf injury but as it wasn't running related and didn't hurt during running so I carried on, aware that it could be a problem.

Fortunately I managed to put in 3.5 miles, equalling my personal best which is limited due to the fact I only have 45 minutes for dinner. That includes the drive there, stretching and the drive back. I thought to myself after the run - I've effectively done a 5k in my lunch break. Although there were no crowds or awards, I was pleased with what I achieved.

There are two good reasons why I drive to the spot I do every Tuesday and Friday - firstly, the route is exactly 1/2 mile so I can accurately measure how far I'm running (I may have number OCD, but seven different doctors have told me sixteen times that I don't have it) and secondly because *this* is my view:

The path is fairly quiet and at the junction to the main road there is a small farm called 'Little Content Farm', something I've never noticed before that made me laugh. Not only does it highlight how small and agreeable it is but it acts as a deterrent to burglars, boasting how few objects are contained within. What can I say, I have a strange sense of humour.

SUNDAY, 29 JULY 2012

Challenge Accepted

It's been a busy weekend. Yesterday I was invited to take an eating challenge in The Rodney Inn, Helston - a 'Man vs. Food' burger. It's fairly new but, until we got there, it was undefeated. The bun featured two homemade beef burgers, sliced cheese, two rashers of bacon, two jumbo sausages and onions and is served with potato salad, salad garnish and chips. Three of us took the challenge on and it was almost defeated by two of us but for a piece of bread and a spoonful of salad.

I managed to become the first person in Helston to consume it all, although I was in two minds as to whether I should have done it at all. Afterwards I was in one mind - absolutely. They even threw in a free desert and a creme de menthe. Lovely. Tea last night came at 8pm and consisted of one piece of toast and marmalade. Those completing the challenge pay half price, so six quid for a day's worth of eatin' is alright by me.

Today I planned an extended run, mapping out a course that was local and I thought I could achieve. It incorporated my usual Tuesday/Friday route so I had a bit of familiarity and I reached a new personal best of five miles. This is good news as there's a 10k in September that I'm seriously considering entering and this is confirmation that I'm likely to get through the course.

Incidentally, I'd like to answer a few potential questions from people driving past me earlier.

1) I saw you walking earlier, so how can you say you ran five miles?

Yes, I still take regular walking breaks. When it comes to the marathon next April, I'll feel the same - if I want to walk for a bit, I will. As long as I cover the distance I'll be happy. Today was about covering more than 3.5 miles and included hill training as well as familiarising myself with a new route. It was also wet underfoot, although that's technically irrelevant.

2) ...but...walk...you were...I saw you...

Yep. You did.

3) ...but...

Absolutely.

TUESDAY, 31 JULY 2012

Hard Times

I never thought I'd find it difficult to run 3.5 miles after running 5 miles but the latter was only two days ago so I'm wondering if I've run too close to my last one. It wasn't terrible, my legs are just aching more than usual and I'm feeling more tired. I'm pleased I got 3.5 miles under the shoes though I'm more pleased that I now have two days off.

In that time I have the option of either biking, rowing or neither so I'm going to stick with my original plan and see how my body feels before deciding. There's nothing worse than starting a run feeling knackered and coming out the other end feeling worse.

FRIDAY, 3 AUGUST 2012

I Am The British Summer

Since I started training back in May I have only ever run in the rain once. This is despite me having a strict schedule, not because I look outside and refuse to run if it's soggy. We've had all those reports of rain and flooding recently, yet I've enjoyed dry run after dry run. This was set to change today as it poured down ten minutes before my run, however the second I stepped out of my car it stopped.

This makes me think I am solely responsible for the sunny periods of each day (not, as you may be thinking, for the rain when I don't run). With this in mind I will run more often if I get some good donations - click the link above. If we continue to have bad weather, think about how you could have changed it and not ruined your barbeque by simply sending a couple of pounds to charity...

SUNDAY, 5 AUGUST 2012

My First 10k

I planned for a 6 mile run this morning which was postponed due to my Mum's birthday party. Had I not attended I would have been killed, rendering me just about useless for future training and events, hence I went out at 4.45pm. I was full of food, full of cake and less hydrated than I should have been yet I was still feeling pretty positive.

My first half mile was cut short as I ran through a field where two Doberman dogs were being exercised and the vision of them bearing down on me was too much to allow me to keep going. I've been advised to stop and walk if dogs start chasing me or seem like they might so I took my self preservation seriously and walked for a bit. After the field the coast was clear so it was full steam ahead along the intended course. It seemed everyone was having a BBQ which made the first section even worse.

I learned a few lessons along the way - six miles is not five miles in the same way that five miles is not 3.5 miles, so my warm down and stretching were much more important and needed to be more intense. I also tried out a couple of energy supplements that gave me a massive stitch after mile two and left me running half a mile in the same condition. Eventually it wore off and I was able to run more comfortably.

I also learned that grey trousers look somewhat suspicious after a six mile run when your sweat runs towards your upper leg areas. Further to my last post we had a massive downpour at around midday that had more than receded by the time I went out and I was running under a hot sun, so I didn't run in the rain once more and was sweating profusely by the time I got home. It was a very welcome shower that I jumped into.

I managed to run 6.5 miles which is slightly more than Mo Farah achieved last night and got a Gold Olympic medal for. How many people can say they did that this weekend? Also I had hills to contend with. I will say, however, that I was a touch slower than Mo so he can keep his well deserved medal.

Mo Farah started the London Marathon in 2013 with the intention of only doing the first half. This gave him a chance to gauge the difference between the 5k and 10k events he did and marathon courses. He stuck rigidly to this plan, coming away from the course at the 13 mile mark. After this he was bombarded with messages from people who had completed the marathon suggesting they had beaten him as they went the whole distance. This made me feel bad for writing this post as Mo is a top athlete and has achieved so much in his career with, potentially, so much more to come. Sorry Mo..!

TUESDAY, 7 AUGUST 2012

Tiny Niggles

I had to cut short my 3.5 mile easy run today as I am most likely still recovering from the weekend, so I ran 1.5 miles before my legs started to ache and I walked the final half a mile back to the car. I will now rest until at least Friday when I'll see how they're feeling and decide whether to rest up some more.

Rest rest rest...

Although I did manage to get out in the rain earlier at last.

FRIDAY, 10 AUGUST 2012

Further Niggles

It seems the pain is here to stay for a while so I got out for a 2 mile run and followed it with half an hour on the exercise bike as it meant I could keep my stamina training up and rest my broken muscles at the same time. This is clearly something I need to keep an eye on.

I had the perfect weather for running as it was ultra clear and sunny but with a bit of a breeze to keep me cool. My legs seem to have taken to the shorts alright and I can now work on getting a bit of a tan before the clouds hide the sun away for good, probably next week.

I'm hoping to be injury free for my training on Sunday, otherwise I may start to get behind and that's never a good thing when you have to carry around so much extra baggage. Training itself is tough but getting out after a break can be even tougher.

I never did get a tan.

SATURDAY, 11 AUGUST 2012

The Agony

Currently my legs are trying to decide whether the side of my shins is going to hurt more or the front. Either way tomorrow's training is going to be tough but, due to the nature of the pain, I've been advised not to rest it (by Runner's World, no less). Tomorrow will be a day of kicking my shins to death in a bid to make them stronger. Wish me luck.

SUNDAY, 12 AUGUST 2012

Injury Part XIII

I went for a tentative run along a stretch I don't know just to keep my muscles warm and used to the exercise, actually getting out of breath for the first time this week and coping with the pain much better. I took it easy, walked when I needed to and got as far as I could before turning round and walking back, stretching my legs as I went. This week I'll be staying off my legs completely, cross training on my usual training days and building myself back up to the 6 mile mark after resting.

I never thought I'd get frustrated at being unable to go for a decent run but it's hit me harder than ever and it's almost taken over my every thought. I'm glad to be recovering slightly and I won't risk anything by over-working myself, keeping to the strategy I first developed at the start of my training by listening to my body. What's that, body? We need a sandwich? Good shout.

TUESDAY, 14 AUGUST 2012

I'm Back

I sneaked off for a crafty 3.5 mile run without telling my legs or my brain just to see if my legs could take it as they've felt a whole lot better since Sunday and the good news is I am completely pain free. This may be for a number of reasons that I'm going to keep a look out for in future.

Firstly, my last run was around 2.5 miles which means it was then followed by a 2.5 mile walk back to the car. I took the opportunity to really stretch my legs as I walked, concentrating on my shins and calves. When I got back I had a hot, deep bath and gently massaged them, keeping off them for the rest of the evening.

Secondly, I've been wearing some less supportive socks for my shorter runs and felt today that my expensive socks (see post on 21 May) were offering more support during and after my run, so I'm now using my new cheap socks purely for lounging around in. I won't take them running again until I'm sure they weren't contributing towards my pain.

Thirdly, it's been over a week since I did my 6 mile run. It may be that I trained too soon after it and need to take an extra day off when extending my runs. Naturally it could be all three or none of these things but they're all possibilities that I need to consider. All this aside, I'm ecstatic to be back to running easy 3.5 mile runs without any discomfort.

SUNDAY, 19 AUGUST 2012

Second Race

I haven't trained since Tuesday for two good reasons; I had to pack for my holiday on Friday when I normally do my easy run and I was trying to catch a new race in Wales in the town we're on holiday in. To achieve this I had to leave Cornwall at 3am to be in Machynlleth for midday yesterday. Only bizarre early morning traffic or my incredible ability not to wake up could have stopped me.

I made it in plenty of time and registered early before getting back to get changed. I'd been told about the run by my cousin Arwel and he was also running, although he's recently achieved a half marathon with a big incline so I couldn't adopt him as a running partner for the race. This race also had an incline, 690ft of incline, which made it completely different to anything I'd trained for.

Due to wet weather the steepest part of the course was deemed too dangerous to run down so the route was reversed, meaning we ran up a hideous slope first off to the summit before reaching the flat and eventually running downhill towards the finish. It was a very hard race but worth the views and experience despite coming back muddy and wet which doesn't ever happen when I'm road running. I also have a new number, something I'm starting to become a collector of.

The rest of the week will be spent running flat road routes to continue my training from where I left off. My next race is in September and is the first of my 10k races. It will also be the first race that will have the same surface as the marathon as my last two have been track and fell races.

THURSDAY, 23 AUGUST 2012

Holiday Training

After the race on Saturday I had to take a look at my training schedule, although it's also because I'm on holiday with the family and their time has to come first. With this, I managed to get out for a very brief run on Monday and have just completed a four mile run with Arwel.

It was a nice, smooth run with amazing scenery and a brand new pavement linking the nearby village to the town we're staying in. This makes it easy to plan longer routes while I'm up here and I can try for five or six miles on Sunday when I next go out. I'll also be getting a swim in somewhere during the week, although it doesn't count as cross training if you spend your time in the pool chasing after children keen to splash you in the face as they're escaping.

MONDAY, 27 AUGUST 2012

Hills And Valleys

Today was my last chance to run with Arwel and we went out in style, running 6.5 miles to a peak of 564ft across the mountains and finally through the valleys in the pouring rain. It started out bright, however the wind soon picked up and brought the clouds with it. The sheep didn't mind and one even had a black eye so there was no reason for us to complain.

The hills were tough but we persevered (read 'I persevered, Arwel waited like a gentleman') and were rewarded with the stunning views and a long downhill section that was bliss by that point. We had to wait for a tractor at one point but once he'd finished and covered us in hedge we were gone again. Getting back tomorrow means a return to my normal training but it was good to add another race and some stunning scenery to the memories of runs gone by.

FRIDAY, 31 AUGUST 2012

Gadgets

With an easy 3 mile run planned today (N.B. easy going, not that I find it easy) and with a recommendation from Arwel, who is now 300 miles away and therefore unable to come running with me so often, I signed up to Endomondo. This is an app that tracks your speed, route and time so you can see how you're doing and compare runs.

Unfortunately it relies on GPS and, thirty minutes after starting my three mile run, I got back to the car to find I hadn't turned the GPS on. This meant my phone recorded me going 0 miles and taking half an hour to do so. Fortunately I rely on other services to check the length of my runs so I could confirm it was definitely three miles on a circular route.

SUNDAY, 2 SEPTEMBER 2012

Quiet Sunday

I managed to work out the running app and put the GPS on this time so I went out with a route in mind and immediately ran into problems (excuse the pun). My shins were aching and felt cramped, although it was nothing I couldn't run through and found that once my muscles were warm I could run fairly comfortably and went on, watching the battle between my legs and lungs intensify.

I was pleased to notice that both were giving me a break for a change, most likely because I went for three miles on Friday and I altered my route to allow a little extra mileage while keeping me within distance of my house in case of injury. When I got back I was soaked and tired but not completely knackered and my phone informed me I'd been 9.5 miles (look at me, chucking away 0.07 miles like it didn't happen) which I was ecstatic about.

Getting back was definitely bliss but it's good to know I'm making a little progress and I can certainly run further than I could in May when I started.

FRIDAY, 7 SEPTEMBER 2012

Post Nine Point Five

This week has been spent recovering from my Sunday run so I went for a brisk walk on Tuesday and was back to running again today, covering my normal three mile route and taking note of how my legs were. It looks like they're back to full strength and my training can continue as normal.

I have a limited training program between now and next Saturday when I have my first 10k race as I want to be as fresh as possible for it. I'm not bothered about what time I achieve or what position I finish in as long as I actually finish. That's been my aim all along and it's worked a treat so far.

SUNDAY, 9 SEPTEMBER 2012

Cross Training. Hungover.

Yesterday I was in the unfortunate position of having agreed to two separate drinking sessions, one a birthday party in a house and the other a leaving party in town. Foolishly I not only agreed to both but went to both, meaning I started drinking at around 6pm and finished at 1am despite knowing that I should at least limit my alcohol intake during training. Something tells me the tortilla chips I used to cure my hangover weren't the best thing for my body, either.

With that I decided to reduce my four mile run to an hour on the bike, adding 30 second sprints every five minutes to maximise my workout (or whatever sporty types might say). An hour was somewhat optimistic though as I made it to the 30 minute mark having done the sprints and then cut them out in favour of a gentle cycle, reducing my overall time to 45 minutes and dragging myself off the bike and into the shower afterwards.

I now have just one run left before my first 10k next Saturday and may have to squeeze in a short one or two miles somewhere along the way to keep my legs strong. Whatever I manage, one thing's for certain; I won't be drinking this week.

TUESDAY, 11 SEPTEMBER 2012

The Last Post

This is it; my final post before the Jurassic Coast 10k on Saturday. I have limited my week's training to include four miles today and perhaps a mile or two on Thursday, although I may forego this training and have a nice sit down and a cup of tea instead. Either way it's all systems go for Saturday save for an unintended lie in or getting run over in the meantime. I even have my number already, although that just means I could lie and say I did it anyway. I won't because I regard you all too highly, I promise. If I succumb to unconsciousness for too long I'll be honest.

Today's run was nothing short of eventful as we were stopped for directions and then passed a car with two occupants both wearing what looked like inflated lifejackets. It's tough running when you're laughing so hard but my training partner and I persevered until we couldn't take it any longer. Our time for the four miles probably wasn't anything to write home about, though we have our reasons. We thought it was a nice quiet country lane we were running down, too...

MONDAY, 17 SEPTEMBER 2012

Hard, Hot And Fast

I entered last Saturday's Jurassic Coast 10k to get some race experience and, boy, did I get some. Thursday and Friday were spent resting up with yet another bout of tonsillitis which meant I had to run with a nose full of phlegm and a throat full of razor blades but when sporty types cross the finish line and comment that it's a tough race you know you'll have little chance of breezing through.

Here's a full list of excuses:

1. Tonsillitis. I've mentioned it before but I feel it's worth mentioning again. I was ill.

2. Heat. We started the run at 11am and I was still going by 12pm on what was one of the clearest and surely hottest of the year. This is not a statistic, purely the feelings of a chubby non-athlete running under the sun.

3. Water. They had a water station at the 5k mark but, by the time I got there, it was empty. I wasn't the only one getting there post watershed; there were a good few thirsty runners who eventually got rehydrated at roughly the 7.5k mark. It wasn't a massive deal, nobody suffered too badly but my decision not to take a bottle with me will never be repeated.

4. Terrain. We were advised it was 'multi-terrain' and even told there would be hills, but the hills we came across were not the hills in the brochure. Anyone who's been along that coast will be laughing at me now, however I have done mostly flat training as that's what I'll be coming across in London in

2013. If you want to enter a 10k, definitely stick a bit of hill training in there first as I'm guessing there aren't many 6 mile flat bits in the UK.

That aside I had terrific support from my wife who waved me off and saw me in at the finish line, furnishing me with some much needed water and a banana before driving me off after the event. I also had support from spectators and the other runners, most of whom were suggesting the last 2k were the longest of their lives although we all made it over the finish line. It's also race number three where I was furnished with a quality gift for finishing:

Thanks to the organisers, marshals, spectators and runners of JC2012 for what was an eye opening experience across the stunning views of Devon's south coast. Who'd have thought I'd actually have running medals in my life?

TUESDAY, 18 SEPTEMBER 2012

The Triangle

Ever since I started my job back in 2006 I've heard people banging on about running 'The Triangle', which is a 5 mile route just beside where I work. It's fairly hilly, pretty windy (read 'wine dee', not 'win dee') and just touches the coast before you find yourself doubling back on yourself and finally running beside the road for the final leg. In 2006, had I run that particular route, I wouldn't have made it back without medical assistance and some kind of breathing apparatus.

As it was, last weekend's 10k was far more fierce and it turned into more of a leisurely jog. This isn't me bragging by any means; it was fairly tough going, still hot and my legs were aching afterwards. However, it does put into perspective the importance of training and the benefits of running routes you haven't done before regardless of how hard they are.

I maybe shouldn't have run that far given the length I did this weekend but I was planning for four miles on the flat and thought a five mile hilly route wouldn't do any harm. We'll see tomorrow how my legs feel, although they seem alright at the moment.

SATURDAY, 22 SEPTEMBER 2012

Easy Runs And Auctions

Yesterday was a very busy day for this fat guy. In the afternoon I went for a three mile run on my normal stretch and found it to be the easiest run I've ever done. It wasn't too hot, there were no hills and I was up for the run with very few walking breaks so I found myself achieving good times for all three miles. I got back to work after lunch and still felt good, a quick walk being enough to stretch them out and stop them from aching.

The evening brought my first fundraising event, an auction of 56 items including a Cornish Pirates match shirt, Signed England shirt, signed DVDs and vouchers from local businesses. I was hoping for £500 from the auction as the lots were fantastic, however we had only five people at the 7.00pm start and had to delay it until 8.30pm when there were around twenty people. Fortunately those who turned up and those who bid beforehand were good enough to raise £1200 between them, not just on the auction but the raffle and the leg waxing too.

This puts me in a good position, chasing just £200 before April having only put together one event. It looks like London is well in my sights and the training can now take priority.

SUNDAY, 23 SEPTEMBER 2012

Training Prep

It had to happen. After a great run on Friday I was due to come crashing down and I did so in style tonight. There may be a few reasons for it as ever, however I planned a four mile run and found myself having to walk from mile two and a half. I'm sure the exercise will do me good in the long run but I could probably have helped myself. Here are the candidates for 'why my legs are killing me now':

Eating too close to exercising - I had a big meal around an hour before going out. Not enough time to digest it meant I was carrying it round with me and it was doing very little for me. This was partly due to me having a busy day and having to cram some exercise in somewhere, opting for the rowing machine initially but abandoning that idea as I've bruised my hand quite badly. Not clever.

Not preparing - Normally on a Sunday I know when I'm going out and get lots of water into me and stretch beforehand. I did very little stretching as I had to get the running out of the way, something it's basically not advisable to do. Training is there to build you up, not get in the way, so next time I'll have to plan it better.

Running too close to another run - This may seem an odd one and an issue I don't get often but Friday I pushed myself quite hard as I felt so good about it. This is equal to doing a longer distance and I definitely should have put in some cross training on the bike.

Cold weather - Until now it's been warm for every run so warming up wasn't an issue. It's not freezing outside and I may be jumping the gun with this one, however it may be something to consider so I'll keep an eye on it.

All in all I'm glad I got out but now wish I'd prepared properly as I have done before. It's been a busy day but I know I need to keep room for my training. I'm hoping the post run regime of a hot bath and leg massage will cure what ails me.

FRIDAY, 28 SEPTEMBER 2012

Upper Body Work

After my usual three miles today I felt it necessary to do a little upper body work. Fortunately for me my Dad's house needed stripping on the outside so I had four hours of SDS chiselling to do to supplement my running. The good news about this is that he'll be donating a little more towards the charity page, so I'm only around £100 short for my target next April.

I've also received my 'rejected' magazine from the London Marathon organisers, which simply means I definitely need the golden bond place St John Ambulance have already offered me. I should be getting my running vest and some fundraising tips very soon...

SUNDAY, 30 SEPTEMBER 2012

Listen To The Experts

I'm currently seven months away from the marathon and I'm four months into my training yet I still get some radical and potentially dangerous running advice from people who know people who have done a marathon before. While I'm happy to talk about my progress and past runs of other people I hate to hear really bad advice being dished out as it is nothing short of injury inducing and could really harm those who have not got access to Runners World magazine or a reputable running shop like At Your Pace in Helston.

I am aware that I need to run 26.2 miles to complete the marathon but that does not mean I should be running every day, running 26.2 miles every week or running constantly and cutting walking out altogether. My training plan consists of three runs per week, two short and one extended as advised by both Runners World and the London Marathon organisers themselves. Anybody who has run a distance race has told me I am doing as much as I should be and I have plenty of time to build my distance so, as long as I stick to my training plan and don't ignore injuries, I should be fine.

In fact I took my training plan's advice and went for a six and a half mile run today, exceeding my best time for a 10k distance and feeling great about it when I got back. I was very tempted to put in a ten mile run, however I have recently been carrying a small injury and thought it better to keep to 6.5 as it means I'll be able to put my normal four in next Tuesday instead of resting for most of the week.

TUESDAY, 2 OCTOBER 2012

Winter Hits

As advised I went running in the rain as it will prepare me for my Winter training but I couldn't have anticipated the problems I faced. The rain wasn't heavy, though it was cold and predictably wet and left me freezing as I cut my hopeful four miles to a very sodden three and a half. I think it's time to get a light jacket, some long sleeved T-shirts and to brace myself for tough times ahead; the honeymoon period is officially over.

FRIDAY, 5 OCTOBER 2012

A Change Of Scene

I've been told for a while to change my route to keep the running interesting but I've stuck to my normal routes as I know the elevations and distances well. Today I decided to mix it up a little as suggested and went for a short route that I'm familiar with yet have never run before. I was semi-aware of the elevation and mapped out the route to find the distance, taking the opportunity of my day off to take it steady as opposed to having limited time to do 2.5 miles on a Friday as usual.

As much as it pains me to say it I did find it refreshing to take in different sites on my route. It took me to places I used to walk through when I was younger, many of which I have seen rarely since passing my driving test. I hate to go all nostalgic on you all but it was rewarding to go back and take in the memories of those almost forgotten years.

I also came across the rudest dog walker ever who took her dog to the side of the pavement and looked with concentration at the pavement to avoid my gaze whereas most other people will at least nod. I know it's up to them if they say 'Hello' or not but I didn't half feel like a strangler. At 10am. Beside a main road. Luckily the next dog walker made up for her.

TUESDAY, 9 OCTOBER 2012

Qupdate

I haven't been doing nothing since my last post. On the contrary; I've done one of everything.

On Sunday I used the bike for an hour and today I ran four miles in the rain. I had prepared for the cold by wearing a long sleeved T-Shirt and, by mile 0.4, I was slowly cooking in my own juices. This is an excellent lesson I felt - long sleeved T-Shirts are great for combating the cold.

I still have the 'wearing glasses in the rain' problem but that is going to be ongoing, I'm sure.

THURSDAY, 11 OCTOBER 2012

Bigger, Better Training

As my runs get longer and I adapt to the training I have discovered some harsh truths. Firstly, I wasn't drinking enough water before I started and probably still don't. Secondly, I am coming to the point where I need to look at my nutrition in depth and start to adjust it more severely. Thirdly, I may not be able to drink quite so much this Christmas.

I have therefore split the rest of my training time into two periods to stop me giving up or getting bored. First is the rest of this year, which I will use to wean myself off the fried chicken and hourly pints of ale and continue with my shorter runs to build my base fitness. From January I will start to extend my runs as I was doing previously, trying initially to turn my 10 mile potential into ability and raising this after the festivities.

By doing this I feel I will keep more of a grip on the running and the shorter distances will keep my feet on the ground, then off the ground, then on the ground again. I'm not looking for a good time in the marathon, purely to finish it, and by extending after January I'm giving myself close to four months to reach the right distance.

I'm not getting bored of running, however I'm really feeling it this week and need to take the pressure off or I will end up crashing and burning before struggling through what is essentially a day's running. Stick with me on this.

FRIDAY, 12 OCTOBER 2012

Short Bursts

The great thing about running at lunchtime on a Friday is that I only have time to put in 2.5 miles, which means regardless of how I'm feeling I will always get out there. How does that work? Well, it feels like I'm skiving. It's like getting sent home from work early or finishing a course an hour before time. A quick jog and then I'm done.

Sorted.

SUNDAY, 14 OCTOBER 2012

Race For Wildlife

This ain't no fun run. It ain't no Sunday jog either. This is 10K...

I remembered today why it's not a great idea to buy £100 trainers and then enter races in Cornwall. The Race For Wildlife 10K in Heamoor does what it suggests, raising money for local wildlife charities and being part of the multi-terrain series in the Duchy. Runners from all over descended onto the back roads to take a not-too-hilly route through the gardens of Trengwainton and back round to Mounts Bay School, taking in the breathtaking scenery (again with the scenery...) and avoiding the massive muddy puddles en route.

This was a much easier race than the Jurassic Coast for a number of reasons, the first of which is the aforementioned hills. Secondly there were two water stations and both had water, although that wasn't necessarily JC10K's fault. Regardless, I took a bottle of internal lubricant with me just in case as there can be no problems if you have something with you at all times.

It was also slightly cooler being later in the year and I donned a long sleeved T Shirt, which kept me warm and fairly dry. I also made sure I stuck my 'Proper Job Disco' T Shirt over the top as the good man has paid my entry fees for the year. Standby for the standard medal picture:

This was my last 10K for the year, the next two runs being 5 and 4 miles long. It's a nice distance and one I try to achieve most Sundays where possible, so it's a shame I won't be getting anything for the rest of 'em. I do like the old medals.

Here's a link to the Proper Job Disco site. All races this year have been paid for by PJD and it's only right you see the young man for yourselves. http://www.properjobdisco.co.uk/

FRIDAY, 19 OCTOBER 2012

Free Weekend

I never noticed before how much races affect me - not the actual running, but the build up to them. I'm not fussed about my times or where I come, yet I seem to have this inbuilt tendency to worry about the course, the weather and if I'll actually complete the distance or not despite having run the same distances previously a number of times.

Fortunately I don't have a race this weekend and my normal Tuesday and Friday jaunts have gone well so I'll plan an extended run for Sunday as usual and take it in my stride. No need to keep ahead of anyone or try to catch the people in front, although I have no idea why I do that in races in the first place.

It's great to get a medal as recognition of going the distance but as they start to accumulate I've realised the big one is only six and a half months away and the training is now much more important than the race experience as the latter is achieved fairly quickly. Still, only two more to go before I look at a possible half marathon next year to top it off.

SUNDAY, 21 OCTOBER 2012

Keep Your Head Off The Road

I use social media a lot to interact with other runners and it seems everyone went out this morning when it was dry and sunny and got some great times and distances in. Trust me to wait until the showers hit to trudge out into the wilderness, hoping I wasn't too camouflaged against the black clouds in a T-Shirt I'd worn to stop me from going see through.

I was trying to decide whether to try for another nine miles or whether I should stick to six, considering the latter to be more sensible as I still have a couple of races left to go. However, I felt good when I went out and put in a quality six miles, keeping walking breaks to a minimum and running for as long as I felt comfortable. When I got back I checked my phone to find I'd gone 6.87 miles and tagged a little extra on the end as there's nothing worse than starting a marathon, getting to 26 miles and not being able to do the final 0.2.

The weather did improve and I ended up carrying the cap I was trying out, ever thankful that I have a wick-away cap on the way for my winter runs. I also have a waterproof jacket that I'm eager to arrive; how times have changed.

The main reason for my consistent running was that I had a lot to think about and kept my thoughts off of running, only bringing myself round when I had to cross roads or turn back on long sections. I find my best runs are those surrounded by a lot of other activity and will bear this in mind for future runs, particularly the extended ones.

TUESDAY, 23 OCTOBER 2012

Equipment

Running used to be so easy. I used to slip on a pair of shoes and some special socks and off I went, puffing and panting into the distance. With the ease of pace and longer routes came the need for other bits and bobs, like a sweat band to keep the worst out of my eyes, a bottle of water to keep me hydrated on the go and an arm strap to put my phone and keys in.

This weekend, with winter setting in, I invested in a rain jacket and a wick-away hat to keep me moving throughout the colder, wetter days. Unfortunately I broke them out three days early and ended up overheating on a five mile run today. This is useful though as I know I'll stay warm this winter and the hat is fantastic for keeping my glasses dry while still keeping my head cool.

Just three more miles on Friday to go before my next Sunday race.

I stopped using the hat before too long as it didn't really agree with the amount of heat I was producing. I got round the glasses/rain issue by leaving my glasses at home, too. Blurry objects are better than objects hidden by rain.

FRIDAY, 26 OCTOBER 2012

Wind Chill Factor

Yeah, so guess who had the bright idea of running 3 miles from work to home on the coldest day of the month so far? Not only was it freezing cold but the wind was up and the drizzle felt like small pockets of absolute zero spotting on my skin. I had to take the swimming pool approach of diving straight in and going hell for leather to warm up, although this did result in a personal best mile of 9.5 minutes.

I know I said I wasn't looking at times yet on these shorter runs it's hard not to take a little comparison if it means you can see your development in another way. Progress makes perfect.

SUNDAY, 28 OCTOBER 2012

The Spirit Of Racing

A nice, five mile run around the Flat Lode at the heart of the Cornish Mining district. What more could anyone want? Well, at 10.30am with half an hour to go we were praying for good weather as it was chucking it down and we made our way to the start line under a sky of cats and dogs. Fortunately it cleared by the time the foghorn went off and we made our way under a cloudy sky along the wet paths.

Most of the race was pretty consistent with nothing to report, however I was overtaken by a fellow competitor at the three and a half mile mark who then stopped dead a few steps later in front of a giant puddle. He decided the best way to tackle it would be to climb the bank beside it which was sloped and muddy and I could see him going head first into the puddle so I waded along the side and offered him my shoulder to lean against in a scene reminiscent of the Disney film *Cars*.

He seemed pretty grateful for this and I let him go back in front where he'd been before, following in his path until we got to a downhill section and I picked up a fair amount of speed to finish the race. Sure enough, as soon as we got back to race HQ his friend reported that the muddy smear up the side of his body was from falling in the puddle and we were both glad we hadn't succumbed to the same fate.

It was all done for this, of course:

Not that, I mean this:

One more race and then I'm done. For this year, at least.

TUESDAY, 30 OCTOBER 2012

October: Done.

I'm always being told that training is about consistency. This image is a screenshot from my Endomondo App and speaks for itself.

« SEPTEMBER 2012			OCTOBER 2012			NOVEMBER 2012 »
Monday	Tuesday	Wednesday	Thursday	Friday	Saturday	Sunday
1	2	3	4	5	6	7
8	9	10	11	12	13	14
15	16	17	18	19	20	21
22	23	24	25	26	27	28
29	30	31	1	2	3	4
5	6	7	8	9	10	11

More of the same next month.

SATURDAY, 3 NOVEMBER 2012

One Hundred Percent

I'm pleased to announce that I've reached my fundraising target of £1,625.00 and can now concentrate solely on the training without worrying about having to make more money. Naturally there's more room for further donations but it's relieving to know the pressure's off.

Tomorrow I'll be hitting the road again with an even bigger smile on my face. For the first half mile at least.

SUNDAY, 4 NOVEMBER 2012

Double Figures

Today I went out early (mainly to avoid the rain) and posted my first ten mile run. This was quite important to me as I've done 9.57 miles before but, as we all know, 26 miles is 0.2m short of a marathon. I couldn't extend my runs after that one as I had so many races to do and wanted to stay relatively fit for those so I've kept to six or seven mile distances on Sundays.

The difference between seven and ten is incredible. It's not just the fact that you're running for longer but my hips started to ache and my knees were putting in a bit of a complaint. Also as running is completely mental (sorry, 90% mental, 10% physical or something similar) my lungs issued a formal apology after three miles as they were struggling to begin with but could see I had more on my plate with my aching legs. I had to plan my route and almost gave in too soon when I realised I was two miles from the end, pulling myself up in time before I seized completely.

I have been running more and more recently and cutting out my walking breaks, although I had three very deliberate breaks today at five, seven and a half and nine miles. I'm confident in my running ability now and kept my pace back to allow me to do the distance. I'm aching all over right now though.

SUNDAY, 11 NOVEMBER 2012

Last

'Last' for two reasons. It's my last race if you don't include the two fun runs I have left (which I don't, so you shouldn't either) and, although the race experience has been good and the other runners have been great, probably the last one I'll do. I get a bit stressed before races unnecessarily and they tend to break up my weekends too much whereas training runs start from home and only last a couple of hours so I can fit them in where possible.

Also 'last' to signify coming last. I couldn't pinpoint the root of my stress before races but I figured it's probably because they *are* races and somebody has to finish at the back. Until now I've managed to avoid that, however Runners World had an excellent article that brought up some great points about being in last place. Firstly, you've gone the distance. Next, you've beaten everyone in the world who didn't take part. Probably most importantly for someone like me who's been told I won't ever post good times because of my build, you've got a medal that says you finished and it looks the same as everyone else's.

It's a good feeling coming first, perhaps the best feeling possible, yet if you go into a race without a hope of finishing first then you may as well reap the rewards of digging in and going the whole way. I now have a handful of medals for distances from 1500m to 10km and they all mean the same to me; I had a great time, they induce great memories, however there's a whole lot of running for me still to do. I want to add a half marathon to my collection next year but for now I'm going to stick with what I've got and keep the training consistent.

The race itself was massively hard work and started after a two minute silence to mark Remembrance Day. It was on a beach that was sand in parts and shingle in others, had three pipes to climb over and had a cold, fairly deep river crossing so I was glad to finish and the inconsistent terrain took me back to the Ras Glyndwr in August, just without the giant hills. For the record I didn't come last this time either, though I would have felt better had I done so. Somebody has to have the courage to start and still get to the end regardless.

There are some photos of me before the races on my JustGiving site, most of which were sponsored by Proper Job Disco. Here's the gratuitous number shot:

For those who read my blog and think I'm a benny big'ead for posting these I should reiterate that this is the last one unless I get all sentimental and post my fun run medal next week. Also I’m training damn hard so back off.

Back to training on Tuesday.

SUNDAY, 18 NOVEMBER 2012

The Right Equipment

Regular listeners will know that I was due at a fun run in Bodmin this morning, however you may not know that I was planning on running with my ten year old son. After looking at the map and finding that the actual run is around an hour and a half away I decided it would probably be best to do the same distance but more locally, so we prepared for a mile run under a bright sun.

After getting prepared for the run my wife realised that our son was planning to run in his best school shoes and, after a little interrogation, we found that he'd left his trainers at school. He had a snowflake's chance in hell of running in his school shoes, so I jumped on the bike for an hour instead and we've postponed our run until later in the week.

I noticed a little niggle in my left knee about fifteen minutes in and tried to ensure I wasn't pushing it too hard, finding it disappeared after five minutes or so. That's another one I'll have to keep an eye on, although most seem to settle down fairly quickly.

So no fun run medal, however the family is signed up to this in three weeks:

Run, jog or walk
Santas on the Run
RNAS CULDROSE, HELSTON
Sunday 9th December, 12 noon
Be one of hundreds of Santas on our 2K sponsored festive fun runs! Entry includes a Santa suit and medal!

Can't wait...

TUESDAY, 20 NOVEMBER 2012

Into 'un

After being ill on Friday and the excitement of the forgotten kit on Sunday I finally got back out to do a run, achieving five miles as part of my training guide under what we thought would be rainclouds. The ol' luck of the Lander hasn't worn off though and we found ourselves gently jogging under a fairly wind free and cloudy yet rainless sky.

Not much to say about it other than feeling a little more tired than usual and I felt my lungs working harder as their recovery has obviously been impacted. I'll try not to leave it a week between runs again for sure. Watch this space for when the luck does run out and I report back after running a few miles, getting drenched and having to swim home.

THURSDAY, 22 NOVEMBER 2012

Cold And Wet

Due to missing the fun run on Sunday I gave my son the opportunity to earn a medal by running a mile, citing today as the best day to fit around my busy schedule. As it was we spent the day watching the strongest winds batter the wettest rain against the windows and I decided to leave it up to him as to whether we went out or not.

Children being children (He's ten) he agreed and we ventured out against the elements to make the distance, getting back to the house when my phone said we'd been 0.97 miles and having to go back to make up the difference. Anybody who's ever run with me has noticed this incredible inability of mine to do slightly under my target and I didn't see why my son should be any different.

Arriving back soaked through and cold I presented him, shivering, with a medal. That's all he wanted to go for, which I can't blame him for as he's got me for a Dad. Poor lad. Still another mile in my legs and it's shown me that bad weather is no excuse not to go running, more of a reason to do less miles at a faster pace. Hopefully...

FRIDAY, 23 NOVEMBER 2012

Weight Loss

I had a really good three mile run earlier. Broke a lot of personal bests. Whatever that means.

I finally succumbed to the pressure and weighed myself to see exactly how much weight I've lost since I started running in May. Doctors, it's time to throw away those BMI charts as I have lost the grand total of absolutely nothing. If anything I may have put on a pound or two. You'd never know it to look at me and I've not altered my eating habits so it's likely I've just toned up a bit.

Apparently my frame size is such that I'm not really meant to be a runner so I've probably backed the wrong sport, however the training's going well and the distances are increasing so I'm going to stop weighing myself again and keep going. This was never about being skinny but it's nice to tell people that six months of exercise has left me at roughly the same weight. They stop asking then.

SUNDAY, 25 NOVEMBER 2012

Worst Run Ever

When I first started out on this venture I couldn't run. No modesty, no exaggerating for comic effect, I genuinely couldn't run. I didn't know where to put my arms and legs and my lungs burned after forty seconds. My feet hurt when I got back in and how I ever went out again I will never know. That run was months ago yet today's was much worse than that.

It's my own fault really. I planned to go out for a nine mile run but I seem to have overstretched myself as I'd been proofreading all morning and had to get sorted for line learning and furniture removal in the evening. This left me a three hour slot to go running, although I hadn't had lunch and had to use up the pasta bake that was in the fridge.

I left it an hour after eating as advised yet pasta seems to stay in the system for so much longer and it was a very fast lesson in nutrition. My pasta stitch came on after two miles and engulfed my entire abdomen, relentlessly pushing me until I was out of breath and could barely run on. I took it upon myself to abandon my run and head home, jogging lightly where possible and walking as much as I needed to. My trip home was spent tasting acidic pasta bake and trying to drown it with the small bottle of water I had.

Not only was I in pain from that but my leg caught a stinging nettle at the side of the road on the way back. I haven't been stung since I was a young adult, probably due to a combination of wearing jeans and staying indoors, both of which running has cured, so it was annoying to say the least that I was struggling home with yet another affliction.

I finally made it back and didn't do too badly in hindsight as five and a half miles of a nine mile run is better than no miles. Looking forward I can draw a line under this run on Tuesday and put a decent five miles in so it's certainly not as bad as I first thought when I turned around with my pasta stitch. Next time I'll go out hungry.

FRIDAY, 30 NOVEMBER 2012

Another Return

After coming down with a virus on Monday I was unable to put in a normal training run on Tuesday so, yet again, I had to go out on a Friday having done no other running during the week. This Sunday I'm hoping to increase my distance once more but I may stick to eight miles or so and pitch how far I run to how I'm feeling. It seems to be the earlier I go out the longer I can run so I'll bear that in mind.

All told I put in a good three miles today and am glad that I'm not suffering as a result. It goes to show that training isn't just to build you up for a day - training's for life. Or something similar.

SATURDAY, 1 DECEMBER 2012

Big Fat Changes

I'd always hoped running would never change me but there's one area in which it was inevitable. Last night I ordered a pizza as Fridays are made for takeaway, however my appetite's dropped and we ordered a medium pizza between us. By the end of it we could barely move and any thoughts of a dessert went right out of the window.

Likewise we've just been for a meal at a pub and ordered what we'd normally have had, finding it a struggle and having to go for a walk after the meal just so we could fit back into the car. I stuck to a few pints of ale with my meal as lager now gives me a headache and I don't think we'll eat for the rest of the day.

On another note, congratulations to Paul on his wedding day. I'm guessing he's not going out for a run tomorrow.

SUNDAY, 2 DECEMBER 2012

Half Time

I'm at a crucial point in my training plan as it's nearing the season of mince pies and the cold, wet days are making running a lot less appealing. I was force fed breakfast this morning and hydrated to the max (with water, not carbonated cool beverages - perish the thought) before going out and aimed for around eight to ten miles as it was wet and I'm still trying out my winter wardrobe.

After two miles I knew it was likely to be a good run so I planned to add a few extensions to my route to take my mileage up while staying relatively close to home, remembering to keep the additions linear (there and back) as I find adding trips around a section doesn't add much at all. By the time I made it to mile four I had to take my cap and glasses off as they were just too wet but I felt I may have been able to go up to 13 miles if I took it easy.

By mile ten a half marathon distance was firmly in my mind and, as I started to tire, I kept going by adding some walking breaks every mile and a half and trying to forget the pain in my hips. Worse than that was the fact I hadn't used any vaseline so while my cycling shorts took the pain from my legs rubbing there was nothing to protect my baby feeders. Still I pressed on, even when I got my baby giraffe legs at eleven miles.

I decided to increase my warm down and walked the last half a mile, proving if nothing else that I probably pushed myself too far. However I can comfortably run the first ten miles which is a great achievement and I can draw from the experience of running on tired legs with the knowledge that I can push to thirteen if I'm being chased by really, really slow lions.

I've rung round and nobody's offering a medal for a half marathon they haven't organised so I can't include a shot of that here. I won't be running the same distance this side of Christmas but I'll keep my regular training up to complete my running foundation and plan to extend my runs even further in the New Year. The most important point for me to take away from this is vas' up on long runs.

THURSDAY, 6 DECEMBER 2012

Rest Up

Sunday was a good day but on Monday my knees were killing me and, as it turned out, I wasn't available on Tuesday for my normal run so I've rested up and will be back on the road tomorrow. Sunday is the Santa fun run so I'm taking the family to our local airbase to take a jog on their runway. Hopefully it'll be closed to aircraft.

SATURDAY, 8 DECEMBER 2012

Change Of Scene

I tried a new route this Friday to save me having to drive to my normal running location but I found that the road I was on had too many side roads and not enough pavements, meaning I was looking over my shoulder for most of the run and couldn't get into a good rhythm. I got the three miles under my belt yet high winds also threatened to push me into the road and, judging by my size, they were pretty strong.

Fridays are made for my usual short, flat route so I will stick to it next week.

SUNDAY, 9 DECEMBER 2012

Ho Ho Etc.

This is it, officially the last race of the year and it was inevitably going to be a Santa Fun Run. I took the family and we all donned the essential Santa suits before doing a (reluctant) warm up and then taking to the runway. As it's a training day for me and the run itself was only 1.2 miles I decided I would then run home, to which a large number of people said 'keep the suit on'.

Another four miles later and I was home, extremely hot and grateful of a cold shower. On the way back a good number of cars beeped and waved giving me some encouragement to run without a break. Well, it's hard to hide the fact when you're dressed up at the side of the road.

The event was organised by the South West Childrens Hospice so please make a donation to Little Harbour here: https://www.chsw.org.uk/make-a-donation

TUESDAY, 11 DECEMBER 2012

Nutrition

Today was my first Tuesday training run for three weeks - not because I'm lazy, but because last week I was recovering from my 13 miler and the week before I was ill. It's good to get back into routine, however Xmas Day is on a Tuesday so I may stick in a 13 miler on the Sunday before to carry me over the festive period. It might happen, you never know.

I've been asked a lot about what I'm eating as my body's changing shape (N.B. no weight loss) and the only thing to report is that I'm actually eating more. I don't tend to go nuts on the bad foods, sticking to slightly more healthy options, however I'm also not on the rice cake and grass diet. Like so much in life it's all about moderation, although regular exercise means an increase of the right calories. I'm not going to preach about eating habits here but common sense is appropriate; if you run a mile a week and eat pizza three times a day you won't feel any benefits.

Search online for appropriate nutritional guidelines. It's what the internet was dug up for.

SUNDAY, 16 DECEMBER 2012

Runnin' In The Rain

As I don't use an mp3 player while I'm running my mind picks inappropriate songs for me to run along to, such as The Monkees' "I'm a believer" or The Cranberries' "Linger", pretty much anything I wouldn't normally listen to that can follow me round for two hours. Today, festively, I was treated to "Let it snow" despite the fact Cornish snow is colder and wetter than actual snow. Why that song? Perhaps for the lyrics "Oh, the weather outside is frightful".

That's because the weather was, at best, frightful. The first and last mile were at least dry but still cold while the rest of my run was ruined by constant heavy rain despite the fact I'd dressed for a dry one. My summer luck had well and truly run out as the rain turned to hail on the most open part of the course and, just when I thought I couldn't get any wetter, a nice gentleman in a Mercedes drove past me through a giant puddle that coated me from top to bottom. No wonder I ended up looking drowned.

Ten miles later and I was more than happy to jump into a red hot bath and read a book before realising I had to attend to my left foot which had been aching for most of my run, probably from about mile three. A ten mile run is hard work but aches and pains make every step so much harder. I thought that getting rid of the cold that had stopped me running last Friday was a victory until my foot started playing up. (Incidentally I jumped on the indoor bike instead of running on Friday as it is more gentle and I needed to do something).

Caution: adult section - contains material about nipples. Only read on if you're over 18 and have a strong stomach.

This was the first time I managed to get some Vaseline onto my chest after countless warnings and, I have to say, it was the worst advice ever. Perhaps it was the rain or my ultra prominent yet highly redundant features, however they've never bled worse than after today's run. From next week I'll be wearing plasters over the poor blighters.

FRIDAY, 21 DECEMBER 2012

Season's Greetings

It's that time of year when everyone starts to wind down so I will say to all of my readers have a very Merry Christmas and a Happy New Year. I will keep on runnin' over the festive season and will return in January with more progress reports.

Stay tuned!

My foot injury prevented me from putting a 13 mile run in on the Sunday before Christmas. I was genuinely disappointed about that.

THURSDAY, 27 DECEMBER 2012

The Time Has Gone

I had my first run in over a week this afternoon and I came back with a foot injury once again. Looking at the stats for my previous runs I realised I may have over-run my old shoes and now need to quickly source a new pair, get them on my feet and change my socks as well. That's if the injury isn't a stress fracture, which will require rest. I'm now a bit nervous about the start of my next phase of training.

This has thrown up a magnificent bit of advice - record your mileage, don't ever forget to do it ever and get new shoes well before they're needed.

WEDNESDAY, 2 JANUARY 2013

Ongoing Problem

I'm still struggling with a foot injury. I went to have it X-Rayed and it's certainly not fractured, however the pain's still present so I'm resting up. I've been using the indoor bike to keep my fitness up but I'm looking forward to getting new shoes and running again next week.

There have been times when I wished I didn't have to run, especially when I looked outside and it was cold and wet, but not having the option to run is torture as I have a long way to go before I'm ready for the 21st April. Here's hoping the pain isn't too deep.

FRIDAY, 4 JANUARY 2013

The Tide's A Beach

I know very little about tides, tide times and general beachyness yet I live less than ten minutes away from a beach. I am very ignorant. When the doctor at A&E told me to give my foot a break once in a while by running on grass or sand I decided to check out the local beach as it offers a longer straight than the local woods and saves me tripping over branches or getting chased by wolves. I checked the distance of the beach online and found it to be 2 miles of golden sand with nearby parking and great views:

Unfortunately, thanks to the miserable tide, I was greeted with a treacherous quarter mile with waves breaking onto pointy rocks:

The bit to the left of the seaweed, under the vast expanse of water, is where the golden sand is. This meant running three miles on the road and hoping my foot would be alright as my new shoes haven't turned up yet. Sigh. So far so good, which means on Sunday I'll be doing another short run supplemented with a bit of bike riding. It's all go here, I tell you.

MONDAY, 7 JANUARY 2013

Beach: Take Two

I went back to the beach at low tide on Sunday and managed a whole half a mile before deciding it was knackering, I wasn't doing myself any favours and if I never run on sand again it will be too soon. I felt a little lazy on the return half mile so I stuck a two mile jog on the end for good measure and got home to put in half an hour on the bike, meaning I made three sessions of not very much anything.

The new shoes are on their way and will be here this week however, so I will be back to ramping up my mileage before the big day in fifteen or so weeks. Not long to go now.

FRIDAY, 11 JANUARY 2013

New Shoes

The new shoes got here just in time for my run on Tuesday and it was clear that the support has gone in my old trainers. It felt like I was running on bubble wrap and another three miler today confirmed this.

The great thing about this is that I have a pair of trainers that are still perfectly good for walking around in so my old Sauconys will be with me for the next few months, making them great value for money if you squint and tilt your head to the left. In all seriousness this is not an area where runners can shave money and any distances require a decent set of shoes as I found before Christmas.

I have to look at energy gels and drinks in the run up to the marathon as I don't really need them up to 13 miles but after that I almost certainly will.

SUNDAY, 13 JANUARY 2013

I Am Back

I finally got out for a long run in the new shoes, getting back up to 10 miles in anticipation of stretching the miles in two week blocks with a shorter run on the third week. This should get me to a decent distance just before I need to start tapering, which I haven't properly looked at yet.

The run itself was very agreeable with a good bit of weather shining down, always a welcome addition. I was a bit concerned when the same guy passed me within ten minutes on the same stretch of road, once wearing yellow and riding a bike and the second time going in exactly the same direction but this time wearing a blue coat and walking. Chances are it was two guys with the same beard but it was early on my run so I wasn't too mentally drained. I will keep a better look out for clones in the future.

I was also asked to keep a lookout for someone's keys at the top of the same road, to which I replied 'sure' and carried on running. Then it dawned on me that I didn't have a clue who the guy was and, if I found his keys, wouldn't be able to return them. In my defence I wasn't thinking straight at that point as I'd seen the same guy pass me twice.

I love being back in routine and am looking forward to getting out again on Tuesday.

TUESDAY, 15 JANUARY 2013

Keeping Track

Since I got my new shoes all those hours ago I have been obsessively recording my mileage to ensure I don't over-run yet another pair of trainers. So far they've done 23 miles and, if I make my run on Friday, they will have covered marathon distance within two weeks. I'd like to dedicate this post to the Saucony Omni 11's that have put in so much hard work and effort in the short time they've been involved with FGRAM.

SUNDAY, 20 JANUARY 2013

Going Further

I was going to post on Friday as my shoes made it to 26 miles which is potentially a significant distance. I didn't though. Clearly. Instead I went for a fifteen mile run today and thought I'd briefly mention it in a post, so here it is. Unfortunately I was going to try out some gels and forgot to take them so I had to walk the last mile and a half, but essentially I carried myself forward for fifteen miles so it all counts.

When I got back I was in a bit of pain but, looking back, it was exactly how I felt the first few times I did ten miles so it's a sign of progress. I was also freezing as, although we've missed the snow in Cornwall, the temperature was just right and I passed a good few frozen puddles. The hardest part of winter training must be getting out of the shower after a run though.

Next Sunday I will only be having a short run, perhaps five miles or so to give my body a rest before another two weekends of long runs. This is advice given to me by someone who has done the marathon a few times and found this system worked well. I will be keeping up the five and three mile runs on Tuesdays and Fridays however.

Here's to the next long run...

TUESDAY, 29 JANUARY 2013

Not Long Now

I've completed the final run of January 2013 and, because I haven't run since last Tuesday, it was difficult. Not bone achingly, lung burstingly difficult but harder than it normally is. Oh, and there was a massive wind to run against. I have learned not to take a training day off, although I'm glad I did it twelve weeks before the marathon and not four weeks before.

Yes, it's now less than twelve weeks until I don my running shoes for the ultimate challenge and try not to fall on my face over the start line. In between I've planned roughly six long runs, sticking to the two weeks on, one week off pattern and taking into account the tapering in April. I will still be running on my 'off' weeks but the runs will be shorter and will probably feel more like skiving than running. I can't wait.

SUNDAY, 3 FEBRUARY 2013

Too Much

I think I got my sums wrong. Today and next Sunday were meant to be 16 and 18 mile runs respectively, however I still have eight weeks before I start tapering and I feel like I'm doing too much. I got back from my 16 mile run after spending the last three miles changing from walking to running quite quickly and, if I carry on the way I'm going, I may have no energy left for the marathon.

With that in mind I will stick to the 16 mile distance and try a little more running than I did this week, training up to 20-22 miles in the last few weeks of March. I haven't picked up an injury and it's good to know I can carry myself 16 miles but I feel the distance is too high for the time of year. This will ensure I don't get bored of running too as my times aren't exactly elite.

I managed to use one of the energy gels and established runners were right - they taste disgusting. I didn't feel it really worked as I ran 15 miles a couple of weeks ago and still had no drive at the end of my run, although I have it on good authority that it's more than likely a mental issue with me giving up before I get home. Knowing there's only a couple of miles left is a real come down.

I did a bit of fatigue training today because I had a late night and a giant curry last night so I woke up and was far too tired to do any kind of exercise, not good with a run ahead. I dragged myself around and perked up eventually although I'm still feeling it now. I'm not completely welded to the spot which bodes well for tomorrow, though.

I also have a new pair of trainers, definitely a good thing as my current ones are up to 69 miles. Which ones take me round I have yet to see but it's likely to be the newer of the two pairs.

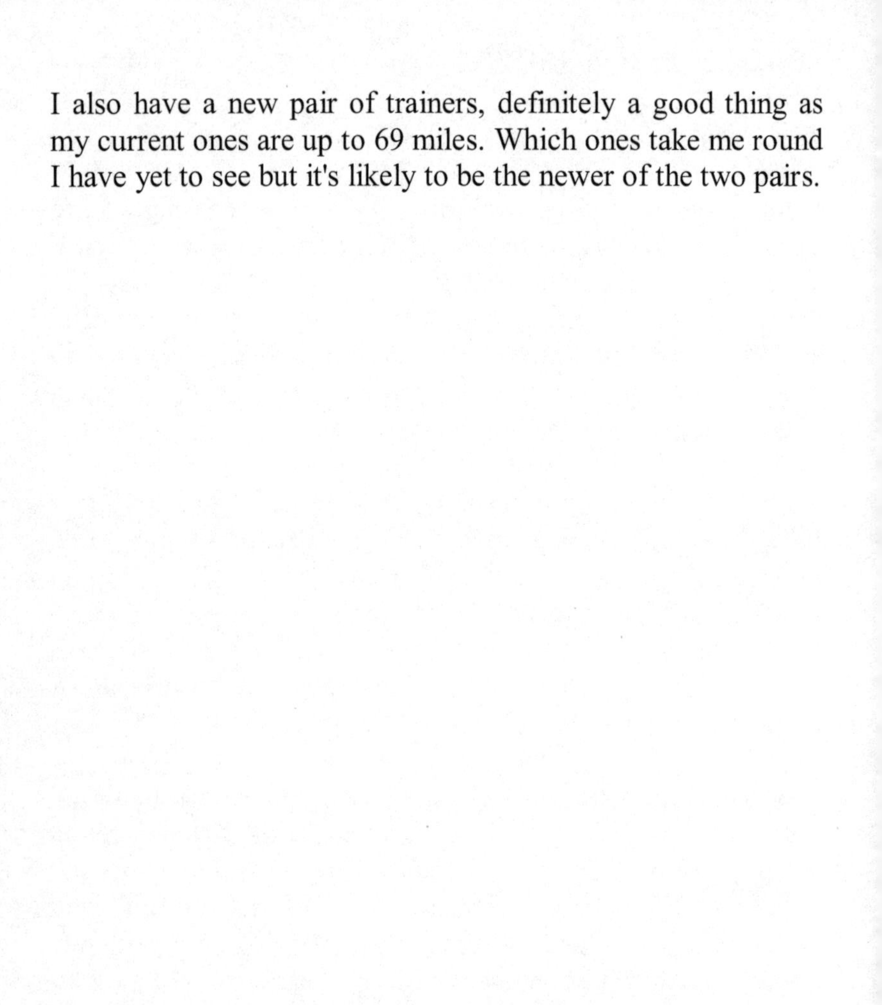

It was actually the older of the two pairs that I wore for the marathon if you were interested. I managed to balance the two pairs quite well and they both had similar mileage by April so I took the pair that felt ever so slightly more comfortable.

TUESDAY, 5 FEBRUARY 2013

Run, Off, Run

The biggest relief of my running career (pause for laughter) so far is that my recovery has massively improved meaning that, despite my 16 mile run on Sunday, I still went out today and put in a pretty solid five miles. It wasn't a record breaking time but wasn't too far off what I do normally so I know that the training I'm doing is sufficient. I still believe I may be doing too much at the weekend so I'll stick to my 16 mile plan this Sunday and go from there.

I also used my new trainers today. They got a bit of mud on them. Gutted.

TUESDAY, 12 FEBRUARY 2013

The Long And The Fast

I had no energy to post anything on Sunday after another 16 mile run as I was frozen, soaked and had thrown in the towel two miles too early and had to walk the last two once again. I don't think this means I can't cover 16 miles, I just think that trying to cover it at the height of Winter makes it near impossible at this stage. I still have a full six weeks of running to go before tapering and I plan on covering bigger distances to get me mentally strong for the day.

Talking of strong, I was convinced to take another route today by a couple of my workmates who go training more regularly than me and keeping up with them was a challenge in itself. I felt good afterwards because I'd worked hard but I doubt I could do the same every week. There's a lot to be said for my 'plod on' method as it's got me up to 14 miles with a two mile, freezing cold walk home afterwards.

SUNDAY, 17 FEBRUARY 2013

Big Oops

Two problems to discuss here. Firstly, after a power run on Tuesday I felt invigorated and went for it on Friday, getting a personal best pace for the first mile. This made me feel awesome until this morning when I went for a shorter, 10 mile run to break up my long runs and felt absolutely terrible. I was tired and aching all over before I'd barely begun and it dawned on me that I went too hard far too close to the big day.

I made it back and barely had time to rest up before we went to Eden for my daughter's birthday party. They have an ice rink there currently and she was keen to use it, however my feet were aching from the run and I ended up with cramp in my foot after 15 minutes. I massaged it to calm it down and got back on the ice for about another 10 minutes before the same thing happened so I stopped and came off the ice a little early.

This has thrown up a couple of great tips - don't get excited and go too fast on a training run unless you're trying to increase your pace (which I definitely am not) and never, ever go ice skating straight after a run. That is, unless your feet are super strong.

SATURDAY, 23 FEBRUARY 2013

What's Update

A couple of things that have made updates near impossible recently. Firstly I'm in a pantomime that opens this Thursday. This means we're rehearsing every day over the coming week and have spent a lot of time already at rehearsals. Secondly we're moving house so any time not spent running or rehearsing is spent packing and moving boxes.

I will return; just know that my training is going as it should...

TUESDAY, 12 MARCH 2013

Been Away

Sorry to regular viewers for the lack of updates recently but I've just moved house (which I'm counting as strength training) and I've only just got the internet up and running. Talking of running...

Last Sunday I went out for a 20 mile jaunt in the strongest wind I can remember encountering, making the whole experience bitterly cold and unpleasant. I managed to achieve the mileage although it took every ounce of my willpower to do so and left me a little sore. I have two more long runs to go before I start tapering as I have a half marathon next Sunday so I will be looking at similar distances for those if possible.

People have given up asking if I walk part of my long distances which is a bit of a shame as I had a great comeback - I achieved 20 miles without gels or water and that included some hills which aren't present on the marathon course. Still, I can keep that in my experience bank for when I've got the crowds beside me and hopefully I won't need to walk at all. I will need to walk. What am I thinking?

I now have a tapering strategy and am looking forward to having shorter long runs of a weekend. After the marathon I have decided to do shorter, faster runs to keep my strength up without taking up too much of my time which can be better spent with my family instead of in my own company. I'm a weird guy to converse with.

SUNDAY, 17 MARCH 2013

'Alf And 'Alf

After running 20 miles last Sunday I looked at my training plan which tells me to do two long runs followed by a week off. This can be spent doing a short run or some cross training, but it is a chance for my body to recover from the long distances and for me to fatten up a bit. I was booked in to Falmouth Half Marathon luckily for me. A day off.

There were close to 500 runners and I realised I hadn't been in a race for a while, although I had done the distance so wasn't half as nervous as I was during my races last year. My plan was to run the entire distance and it took a bit of effort as the hills of Falmouth are long and steep, although my lack of knowledge of them helped me to blindly run to the top before realising how tired I was.

To keep my mind off the running I started to think about breaking the distance up and how I would offer advice to others thinking of the same thing, so here is my quick guide to running a half marathon without trying to break any records or become a pro athlete.

The Fat Guy's Guide To A Half Marathon

Mile 1 has to be your first target. Your limbs have gone from sitting in a warm environment to carrying your body weight and they get absolutely no advance notice of this as the only thing your brain will do is tell them to move. This can be distressing for them, so getting to mile 1 will give them a chance to settle down and realise that they are involved in some activity and need to keep going. It will also get your breathing right and should level the rhythm between your breathing and your movement. Never set off too fast, always stick to your normal training pace as it'll help you to go the distance.

Mile 2 is a terrible target. You want to triple your investment, not double it, and the number 2 is a bitter number; always in the shadow of the number 1 and not willing to do anything about it. Don't feel sorry for cruising past number 2 and, if possible, don't give it a second thought.

Mile 3 is a great second target. When you get there, high five yourself and go nuts for your achievement. Probably best to do it in your head as you don't want to scare the locals but you should put your mental effort into how well you've done. Another great thing about this point is that we are all taught how to manipulate 10 when we're in school as it's a simple number to perform with mathematically. 3 + 10 is…you've guessed it…13, the total number you're running. You can't help but associate 3 with 10 during a half marathon and 10 is a cuddly, round number used by happy mathematicians all over the world.

High fiving yourself mentally is a great boost and you may pick up slightly at this point, although consistency is important. It's not unusual for that mental pick up to sail you past mile 4 without you noticing and the next target, through no fault of your own, is mile 5. Like 10, 5 is an easy number to work with. If you're given 9 of something to share with a mate, you'll take 5 as it's roughly equal. Likewise you'll take 5 of 11 items given to share. Everyone is attracted to 5 and by now you'll be feeling like you've always run, like you were born to run and like you can't imagine never running. Possibly.

Mile 6 is a superb target for the same reasons; splitting things into two. After mile 6 you'll come to the mid-point of the race and, by not knowing exactly where it is, you'll take yourself to mile 7 looking for it. By the time you get to 7, you'll have realised that you've already passed the half way mark and it is now harder to turn back and quit than to keep going.

Mile 8 comes off the back of the half way euphoria and is often overlooked because of this. Don't feel bad, though. If you hit a rock with a stick enough times the rock thinks it's normal and that's exactly how number 8 feels. It'll watch you pass by without expecting a nod and a doff of the cap, not caring either way if you're there or not, unlike your next target.

Mile 9 is just one mile away from mile 10. One mile is nothing in the great scheme of half marathons and we all remember the attraction of the number 10 so by this point you'll be aching but keen to press on. Your old friend is just around the corner, ready to help you multiply other numbers by itself simply by adding a nought on the end.

Mile 11 is a strange fellow. It's a skinny number and can be missed because of this, although it refuses to eat pies to fatten up. Who wouldn't eat a pie or two every now and then? This fat runner would. Stay away from number 11. It's hiding a weird secret.

Mile 12, one mile from your finishing point, will always be welcomed for that very reason. Another chance to high five yourself internally, this point is where the crowds start to form and root for you. They'll call out your number, clap and tell you to keep going while they sip hot drinks. They want you to succeed. They know you don't need them running to do it.

Mile 13 is a sneaky little fellow. Whenever you say 'half marathon' you think 13, people say 13 and you both agree 13. 0.1 mile is still lurking beyond 13, though. Would you stop 0.1 miles before your house and tell people 'that's close enough'? That last little bit should only be on your mind from about mile 12 as it's better off hiding in the shadows, however it should not be forgotten after this point as it exists and must be run. Nobody ever caught a fish by sweeping the nets 0.1 mile away from the nearest school.

Once you get over that sacred line keep moving and stretch your limbs. Grab a drink to sip and get some food down you as you start to think about putting on some warm clothing that you should have at the finishing point. You've done extremely well but you have to listen to your body and be ready to give it what it wants. If this is your first half marathon your body won't be used to the mileage and will start to cool down quickly. I always make sure I have something dry to step into after a long distance, particularly if I'm away from home.

Enjoy!

THURSDAY, 21 MARCH 2013

Exhaustion

I am tired. There, I said it. Not only did I have the half marathon last weekend but I ran 20 miles the weekend before and have moved house and finished a pantomime recently. It would be great to be able to concentrate solely on my training but, as ever, life gets in the way and I have to co-ordinate myself efficiently.

This means that instead of running tomorrow lunchtime I jumped on the bike for a bit of cross training tonight. It will give my knees and hips a rest as well as perking me up a bit for the weekend when I attempt 20 miles again. A couple of early nights will help, too. Hey, giving up late nights and copious amounts of beer is something I had to do a little while ago.

I feel a little better knowing I only have two more big runs just over a week apart, although I know I need to start working on my taper and watching for injuries. It's been relatively pain free on the injury front so I can have few complaints.

London is in my sights. April 21st, one month away...

MONDAY, 25 MARCH 2013

Twenty Times Two

I've just completed my second ever twenty mile stint, although I must admit I should have taken gels this time as I now only have one long run left to get it right. I'm hoping my day-to-day nutrition is alright as I seem to be able to go the distance without any top ups but for comfort I think a gel or two would help.

Next week is my last long run before I taper so I thought I'd share what I've read about this time. Essentially a runner cannot improve their fitness during the taper period, which for the marathon I've taken to be the three weeks before, so it's important to take it easy and reduce the length of the runs. Everyone has a variation on their training plan but luckily the taper plan works on percentages.

Tapering begins after your last big run which should be around 20 miles three weeks before the marathon. After this drop your mileage down to about 70-80% for the first week, 50-60% for the second week and 30-40% for the third week. This means for *all* runs, including the short ones. Keep eating as much as you're used to and expect to put some weight back on, most of which will strip off during the marathon itself.

Also don't do anything too tiring during this period and cut out the strength training (if applicable, though not in my case). The most important thing during this period is getting your legs to the start line, preferably attached to the rest of you. Your legs will get twitchy, you'll feel new pain but remember why you're doing it in the first place.

MONDAY, 1 APRIL 2013

Easter Sunday

There is very little that can get in the way of training if I want to do the marathon comfortably and that includes Easter. This Sunday I ran my last training run of 20 miles and I have to admit I'm starting to get sick of it - sick of the time it takes, sick of the pain afterwards, sick of the constant wind and chill on my joints, even sick of the water I have to drink.

After yesterday's run I bought 4 pints of skimmed milk and went through 3 of them before I went to bed, grateful for the change in taste. Fortunately all of my complaining is redundant as my next two long runs will be 14 and 10 miles respectively and I am still looking forward to the marathon despite the distance.

I thought about how ready I am and, while I was returning yesterday, I imagined being offered an extra 6 miles in return for never having to run again. Had the deal come about I would definitely have gone for it and carried on. That's not to say I won't ever run again after the marathon but it will be fantastic not to *have* to run every week.

I'm tired, I'm grouchy and I can't even appreciate the fact that I've done my last long run. Running's easy though isn't it? One foot in front of the other.

SATURDAY, 6 APRIL 2013

15 Days To Go

I'm finally into the tapering phase, the bit of my training I've genuinely been looking forward to. However, I went for my usual three miler yesterday and very nearly went over on my ankle. For the next two weeks I'll be running so cautiously it will probably take me twelve hours to do my 14 mile run tomorrow, but if that's what it takes to get me to the start line then that's what I'll do.

Had I gone over I would have wasted ten months of training, one month of doing three 20 mile runs and been shot in the head behind a big screen like the four legged runners of the Grand National. Well worth avoiding.

SUNDAY, 7 APRIL 2013

Arrogance

I realised earlier that I may have come across as a little arrogant in the last week because I told people I was looking forward to an easy run of 14 miles. I should stress that the 'easy' part is comparable to the last month spent thinking about having to run 20 miles every weekend and the shorter distance simply meant I could actually go out and enjoy my running once more as I knew I would be able to recover more quickly.

As it was this improved attitude towards my run meant I ran a little faster than usual and made a personal best time for a 13 mile distance, a bit of a non-achievement but a happy bi-product of going out. Regardless, I have been more aware of my surroundings and have been certain to avoid anything that might rip my foot off and throw it down the road.

With only one more long run to go I am now completely focused on getting round the marathon circuit, however I'll be sure to keep updating this site and suggesting you pour your spare cash into my JustGiving site.

As a small side note, a number of people have asked if I will keep running after the marathon as it would be a shame to waste all the training I have done. I don't see it like that; I have been training to partake in a specific event and, even if I don't make the marathon for whatever reason, I have run over 500 miles since this time last year, 94 of which were in the last month alone. I will endeavour to continue, but I didn't get fat by being proactive. I can only hope.

SATURDAY, 13 APRIL 2013

Less Exercise

As predicted by the experts I am missing running like I never have before. I had to cut my Tuesday run to 2.5 miles and Friday to 1.5, the latter of which I didn't have time for so I have more pent up energy than a shaken can of energy drink in a car with no suspension going down a road with no tarmac etc.

I'm also taking on carbs as suggested and next week will be getting 70% of my calorie intake from pasta, potatoes and rice. This sounds like I have done extensive research but really I found three articles that said the same thing and figured they must be right.

Despite taking all this energy in and not being able to expend it in a manner I've become accustomed to I am following advice not to start too quickly next Sunday and to stick to the pace I've trained to. All is set in the world of fat marathon training and the most important thing now is to get registered at the expo and get to the start line in one piece.

Ready, set, waaaaaait...waaaaaaaait...

MONDAY, 15 APRIL 2013

Training Complete

I was meant to be running 10 miles yesterday but I barbequed for three and a half straight hours instead. However my legs weren't going to let me give up that easily and I combined my Sunday and Tuesday runs to visit my training haunts, covering the road to Gunwalloe and the flat, straight road with the great view I first ventured on to eleven months ago. Incidentally, the latter was where I saw the fox (ahhhh) with the rabbit in it's mouth (urgh). As ever life went full circle and I saw a baby rabbit running beside me along the road before darting into a bush.

You'd think with all that training behind me I'd know that I can't get away with not putting plasters on my nipples when I do a 10 miler and got back in time for both lefty and righty to glow bright orange beneath my T Shirt. This has led me to sum up training in three simple words - experience, consistency and determination. Custard Creams are also important.

So to Sunday, where 55,750 people will line the streets, 36,000 mass runners will don their vests and I will join them (with a T-Shirt underneath), watching intently as they all run past me and the marshals clear up the road behind me. I have to get it done in 8 hours to get a medal, although covering the distance will be a real measure of how far I've come in the past year.

This week will involve a lot of chilling out, putting my feet up and trying not to get run over.

WEDNESDAY, 17 APRIL 2013

Paved With Gold

I'm packed for London and have little access to the internet between now and Sunday. I will be sure to come back and tell you all about it. Until then, goodbye and keep your eyes on the pies.

WEDNESDAY, 24 APRIL 2013

Running The London Marathon 2013

It's been three days since I ran in London and I've thought and spoken of little else since, purely due to the enormity of the task in hand. In eleven months I have gone from absolutely no running to one of the most recognisable events in the running world suffering blisters, foot injuries, shin splints, chafing and a gut wrenching pasta stitch. They are bored to tears of me talking about it at work, though.

The journey up was fairly uneventful despite five and a half hours in the car with my two eldest children, the youngest having been accepted into two friends' families to keep her occupied while we were away. My wife and I had never booked ourselves into a hotel in London and were learning all the time about the transport, number of places to stay and the activities available to us while we were there. Our limited budget meant we had to stay in Dagenham, well away from the city centre, however a quick tube ride meant we were never far away from our destination.

Our first night in London was particularly restless as we were placed underneath a family of elephants who found it amusing to jump from their beds onto their floor which, in turn, was our ceiling. We complained twice, giving them good reason to up the volume well into the late hours and, by 11pm, we'd finally managed to get to sleep in spite of their acrobatics. The hotel was fantastic to us in the morning and the desk operator apologised for a situation that was no more his fault than our local MPs and gave us a refund without asking. They seemed to be camped there for our second night too, although they were a little less energetic and kindly kept the tedious banging to the more normal time of 8pm to our relief.

I had to register for the race at the London Marathon Expo held in the Excel centre. As ever this was well signposted and easy to find, although it would be hard to miss considering the size of the place. I'd read that hanging around the expo is a bad idea as runners can become a little overawed so I got my number and tracking chip and made my way around briefly looking for a running belt that I had failed to acquire during training. I was fortunate to get one for the low price of a fiver, although I later found it was slightly too small for my biscuits. I was genuinely gutted not to have custard creams for the marathon. I did manage to meet up with Paul though and it was great to catch up and talk running with someone who's been there, done it and been supportive right from the very start.

After the expo we made it back to the hotel in time to unpack and watch a little TV to calm down before getting the little ones to sleep. All four of us were cooped up in the one room so it was interesting trying to juggle the different sleeping times but I hope we managed it effectively.

The Saturday before the race, during which I had been advised to put my feet up and relax for the whole day, turned into a seven hour walk around the Science Museum. Admittedly we all had a great time as we didn't want the whole weekend to be just about the marathon, although seven hours walking does nothing good to your hips. We'd planned to do the Natural History Museum as well, deciding it would be best for my wife to take the children there while I raced as our non-familiarity with London meant we didn't know where the best cheering points would be and I knew I would have to focus on maintaining momentum to even have a chance of finishing. I also suggested that watching a fat guy run about for hours might be a tad boring after a while.

That night I tried to think of sausages in onion gravy to keep my mind off the expected six and a half hour run, failing miserably and kicking my wife repeatedly in the process as I inevitably ran in my sleep. It seemed my hips weren't too far gone for that, at least.

On the morning of the marathon we all got up at 5.45am to the first of our three alarms and managed to dress ourselves and get fed despite the tiredness. My plan was to leave at 6.45am to catch the tube around 7.15am, an hour after which I would be walking up to Greenwich Park and saying goodbye to my loved ones for the last time before my longest ever run. Perhaps arriving two hours early was a touch over cautious but I wanted to get there in time for the official St John Ambulance photo at 9.10am. I searched the entire park after dropping my kit bag to the appropriate truck and found no sign of any St John runners, even asking the medics if they knew where I was meant to be. I didn't panic as I knew where I would be starting from, more giant signs showing me the way once again.

I met up with a few St John runners who were all looking for the photo point at the same time, however by the time we found out where it was we were too late. One of my fellow runners suggested that the walk was a good warm up yet I knew it would sound like a poor excuse if I said I'd done the marathon but "wouldn't be in any photos". As it was the photographer kindly took a couple of the lost group and I had a shred of evidence that I'd at least made it to the start.

As the St John crowd dispersed we made our way to our separate pens, each numbered according to our expected finish times; 1 being the fastest runners, 9 being the slowest runners. Naturally I could see everything from pen 9 and the enormity of the event finally dawned on me although I was fortunate not to have any nerves. I was possibly too stupid to be nervous which has yet to be confirmed. This did mean only one toilet visit was necessary before I lined up, apparently an achievement before I'd even started.

It was frosty when we'd left the hotel, the air temperature hovering around 0°C and mirroring our training conditions. By the time we started it was hot, clear and made me glad I'd applied suncream. It did get cloudy later on, although the temperature was still higher than it had been all year.

After the 10am start it took me 25 minutes to get to the start line and, due to the crowds, I walked the whole way in a polite shuffle. Our times were measured from the start line via the tracking chip attached to our trainers, although the marathon livery is all taken down at 6.00pm that night and that left me just over 7.5 hours to do the course. I knew I had a challenge on my hands, not least because medals are only handed out to those who finish in this time but also because they were donating £2 per finisher to those caught up in the Boston Marathon blasts a week earlier.

Due to the number of runners taking part I found the whole course to be more congested than anticipated and that, along with the temperature, made me tired faster than expected. During training I'd managed to run around 14 miles and then started walking but I only made it to the 11 mile mark before I had to give in. This drastically altered my plan as I knew I couldn't walk 15 miles so I geared up to start running again after the 12 mile mark and was back on track.

While I was running I decided I wanted to run as much as possible during both the second half and after the 20 mile mark so I accepted some sweets from a spectator to keep my energy levels high and used one of the gels from my running belt. I'd never used Lucozade much during my training but I took a good amount at each station, again with the intention of keeping my energy up. I was advised not to take a drink at every water station and so only took a few sips from the bottles I did take, keeping hold of them and spreading them over as much of the course as possible to stay hydrated.

I'd spent the Friday and Saturday before the race hydrating and the week before carbo loading so I felt good for the most part of the race, although the pain in my legs, back and shoulders was very much present from about mile 16 and I was in agony by mile 24. I never thought I'd consider quitting yet here I was, 2 miles from the end, trying to convince myself to continue. Perseverance and experience helped me to carry on (as well as some well placed signs from the Lucozade people – "Pain Is Temporary" being one of them) and I made it past the St John cheering point at mile 25 where my wife and children had found my brother and were giving it their all to keep me going.

Mile 25 itself seemed to have vanished off the face of the earth for a while and I wondered if I'd already passed it at one point before finally seeing it in all its glory. That was when I knew I could make it and any doubt from the previous mile was well and truly extinguished. I also noticed I was within my target and that maintaining my pace would give me a better time than anticipated.

It seemed an age before the finish line came into view and the 800m signs were well received. I started jogging for what seemed like the thousandth time that day to the 200m point where I pooled all of my energy and went for a completely unnecessary sprint finish to play up to the crowds that weren't allowed near the finish line. That led to a bit of an anti-climax as I collected my medal to the quiet of a lone tannoy and a few people, certainly not the thousands of voices I'd thought would be there.

My Dad was volunteering for St John at the finish line and he was the first familiar face I saw after finishing, though we couldn't chat for long as he had a casualty to attend to. A lot of people understandably find themselves feeling ill after the race but most people who saw me commented on how well I looked in comparison. Slow and steady may not win the race but it gives you a better chance of surviving afterwards.

My official time was 6 hours, 12 minutes and 3 seconds shaving almost 18 minutes off my predicted time. Within that time I saw a good few athletes being sick where the 22 mile point meets the 13 mile point, (I was on the latter, they were on the former. Regurgitating.) thousands of spectators shouting my name and offering sweets to the runners, a woman on crutches who was more than determined to finish and an array of crazy costumes. At one point someone shouted "Look, it's Percy Pig!" to which I took offence before being passed by a guy in a giant pig costume. I was also passed by the Michelin Man, two guys carrying an apple press, more than a few supermen, the Samaritans telephone (who only made about five minutes on my time) and two members of the Jamaican bobsleigh team – complete with bobsleigh.

After the race I made my way to the St John after party where I met my family and sat down with a cup of tea and some sandwiches. This is a great tip; even if you get a ballot place in the marathon, run for a charity and get some sponsorship. It will save having to travel so far for replenishments after the race. I was also treated to a sports massage and found out the football scores, a vital part of any weekend. I found it hard to eat and drink a lot afterwards but was advised to keep my fluid and salt levels up for 48 hours after the race so I took small mouthfuls and sipped water as much as possible. I was told the most common problem after a marathon is hyponatremia as runners often drink too much and don't replace their vital salts.

I struggled to get comfortable during the night of the marathon as I ached all over and found pain in muscles I hadn't used for so many years. I had absolutely no interest in watching TV and tried to sleep as early as possible, getting to bed at around 9.00pm but struggling to regulate my temperature which also caused me problems. I finally dropped off at about 11.00pm that night in too much pain to really digest any achievement.

We travelled back the next day, my wife driving as I was in no fit state to do so. Unfortunately the sat nav that had so expertly taken me around the centre of London decided we needed a scenic route and took us past a number of iconic London buildings and their associated traffic. By the time we finally made it out we were even more dishevelled and looking forward to the more laid back roads of Cornwall.

My legs and back were still aching quite a bit the day after travelling and it took a good amount of walking around to stop the stiffness. Moving around after the marathon is essential and the same goes for the few days afterwards. Today I feel fantastic and am looking forward to my next run on Friday as I'm sticking to the same training days as before the marathon although I'm reducing the distance of my Sunday runs. I'll be doing more races this Summer, particularly the Jurassic Coast 10k that I found so challenging last year.

I've thought about whether I could have improved my overall marathon time and know that, had I put in an extra midweek long run, I may have shaved a bit extra off. However it's just as likely that I would have spent even less time with my family and would probably have become fatally bored with running so I'm confident I trained as much as possible to keep me going and to get me around the course. Now that I have finished my main running target I can get back to weekends out with my family and even enjoy a few nights out.

Most importantly I've found that you can go from zero to marathon within eleven months if you're consistent with training, heed good advice, ignore bad advice and kit yourself out properly. It's not something you can blag as many have found out to their disadvantage. It's a tough journey but ultimately one that offers a reward that will last a lifetime.

TERRY
St John
47962

St John
Ambulance
TERRY
St John
Ambulance
Virgin money
47962
adidas

local life in a Packet · twitter @thepacket · news

'Fat Guy' runs marathon

By EMMA FERGUSON

emma.ferguson@packetseries.co.uk

AFTER self dubbing it the 'Fat Guy Runs a Marathon' attempt a Helston man has put his weight behind the London Marathon – and come out the other side with a time to be proud of.

Terry Lander, an electrician at RNAS Culdrose, completed the run in a "fat flattering" six hours, 13 minutes and three seconds – almost 18 minutes less than his expected time.

In the process he has raised more than £1,700 for St John Ambulance, with donations still to come in.

Getting into the marathon proved something of an annual tradition and took six years, but 2013 was Terry's year.

He saw himself at the start line – which took 25 minutes to get to, due to the amount of runners – and despite having to contend with surprising heat, flagging energy levels and, most importantly, a lack of custard creams, Terry fared relatively well.

He said: "The marathon itself came on the hottest day of the year so far and, after training in almost arctic conditions throughout the winter, came as a bit of a surprise.

"The marathon organisers put plenty of fluid stations in, which helped a great deal, and the crowds were phenomenal, cheering on people they didn't know and shouting out the names they saw on people's vests which gave us a buzz all the way around.

"The last few miles were so much harder than I ever anticipated – however I finished within my target of 6.5 hours."

His family cheered him on at the end, a familiar face at the finish lane. Adding that due to the number of runners taking part he found the whole course to be more congested than anticipated and that, along with the temperature, made him tired faster than expected.

"During training I'd managed to run around 14 miles and then start walking but I made it to the 11 mile mark before I had to give in. This drastically altered my plan, as I knew I couldn't walk 15 miles, so I geared up to start running again after the 12 mile mark and was back on track," he said.

> *The last few miles were so much harder than I ever anticipated*
>
> *Terry Lander*

Terry has now developed a love of running – although he admits that a full marathon may not be on the cards again anytime soon.

"My family have been amazingly supportive throughout my training and, although my marathon days are most likely numbered, I will keep running short distances.

"I've found that you can go from zero to marathon within 11 months if you're consistent with training, heed good advice, ignore bad advice and kit yourself out properly.

"It's not something you can blag, as many have found out to their disadvantage. It's a tough journey but ultimately one that offers a reward that will last a lifetime."

To still make a donation to Terry visit the charity donation website www.justgiving.com/Lyvit2013.

News

As you can see the papers were all over me.

I recovered fairly quickly after the marathon, getting back to work on the Tuesday afterwards and returning to running the following Friday. I have since maintained my Tuesday/Friday/Sunday routine and have taken in some more scenic routes.